Learning the Unix
Operating System

Learning the Unix
Operating System
Fifth Edition

Jerry Peek, Grace Todino, and John Strang

O'REILLY®

Beijing · Cambridge · Farnham · Köln · Paris · Sebastopol · Taipei · Tokyo

Learning the Unix Operating System, Fifth Edition

by Jerry Peek, Grace Todino, and John Strang

Copyright © 2002, 1998, 1993, 1987, 1986 O'Reilly & Associates, Inc. All rights reserved. Printed in the United States of America.

Published by O'Reilly & Associates, Inc., 1005 Gravenstein Highway North, Sebastopol, CA 95472.

Editor: Laurie Petrycki

Production Editor: Mary Brady

Cover Designer: Edie Freedman

Printing History:

1986:	First Edition. Written by Grace Todino and John Strang.
1987:	Second Edition. Revisions by Tim O'Reilly.
April 1989:	Minor corrections.
August 1993:	Third Edition. Additions and revisions by Jerry Peek.
June 1994:	Minor corrections.
January 1998:	Fourth Edition. Additions and revisions by Jerry Peek.
January 2002:	Fifth Edition. Additions and revisions by Jerry Peek.

ISBN: 0-596-00261-0

[M]   [9/02]

Table of Contents

Preface

The Unix Family of Operating Systems

An *operating system* (or "OS") is a set of programs that controls a computer. It controls both *hardware* (things you can touch, like keyboards, screens, and disk drives) and *software* (application programs that you run, like a word processor).

Some computers have a *single-user* OS, which means that only one person can use the computer at a time. Many older OSes (such as MS-DOS) can also do only one job at a time. But almost any computer can do a lot more if it has a *multiuser, multitasking* operating system such as Unix. These powerful OSes let many people use the computer at the same time and let each user run several jobs at once.

Unix was invented more than 30 years ago for scientific and professional users who wanted a very powerful and flexible OS. It's been significantly developed since then. Because Unix was designed for experts, it can be a bit overwhelming at first. But after you get the basics (from this book!) you'll start to appreciate some of the reasons to use Unix:

- It comes with a huge number of powerful application programs. You can get many others for free on the Internet. (The GNU utilities, available from the Free Software Foundation, are very popular.) You can thus do much more at a much lower cost.

- Not only are the applications often free, but some Unix versions are also free. Linux is a good example. Like the free applications, most free Unix versions are of excellent quality. They're maintained by volunteer programmers who want a powerful OS and are frustrated by the slow, bug-ridden OS development at some big software companies.

- Unlike OSes such as Microsoft Windows and MacOS that are designed for certain types of hardware, Unix runs on almost any kind, from tiny embedded systems to giant supercomputers. After you read this book, you'll be ready to use many kinds of computers without learning a new OS for each one.

- In general, Unix (especially without a windowing system) is less resource-intensive than other major operating systems. For instance, Linux will run happily on an old system with a x386 microprocessor and let multiple users share the same computer. (Don't bother trying to use the latest versions of Microsoft Windows on a system that's more than a few years old!) If you need a windowing system, Unix lets you choose from modern feature-rich interfaces as well as from simple ones that need much less system power. Anyone with limited resources—educational institutions, organizations in developing countries, and so on—can use Unix to do more with less.

- Much of the Internet's development was done on Unix systems. Many Internet web sites and Internet service providers use Unix because it's so flexible and inexpensive. With powerful hardware, Unix really shines.

Versions of Unix

There are several versions of Unix. Until a few years ago, there were two main versions: the line of Unix releases that started at AT&T (the latest is System V Release 4), and another from the University of California at Berkeley (the last version was 4.4BSD). Some past and present commercial versions include SunOS, Solaris, SCO Unix, AIX, HP/UX, and ULTRIX. Freely available versions include Linux, NetBSD, and FreeBSD (FreeBSD is based on 4.4BSD-Lite).

Many Unix versions, including System V Release 4, merge earlier AT&T releases with BSD features. The POSIX standard for Unix-like operating systems defines a single interface to Unix. Although advanced features differ among systems, you should be able to use this introductory handbook on any system.

When we write "Unix" in this book, we mean "Unix and its versions" unless we specifically mention a particular version.

Interfaces to Unix

Unix can be used as it originally was, on typewriter-like terminals, from a shell prompt on a command line. (See the section "Examples," later in this chapter.) Most versions of Unix also work with window systems (sometimes called Graphical User Interfaces, or GUIs). These allow each user to have a single screen with multiple windows—including "terminal" windows that act like the original Unix interface. (Chapter 2 explains window system basics.)

Although a window system lets you use Unix without typing text at a shell prompt, we'll spend most of our time on that traditional command-line interface to Unix. Why?

- Every Unix system has a command-line interface. If you know how to use the command line, you'll always be able to use the system.

- If you become a more-advanced Unix user, you'll find that the command line is actually much more flexible than a windowing interface. Unix programs are designed to use together from the command line—as "building blocks"—in an almost infinite number of combinations, to do an infinite number of tasks. No windowing system that we've seen (yet!) has this tremendous power.

- You can launch and close windowing programs from the command line, but windowing programs generally can't affect a command line or programs you run from one.

- Once you learn to use the command line, you can use those same techniques to write *scripts*. These little (or big!) programs automate jobs you'd have to do manually and repetitively with a window system (unless you understand how to program a window system, which is usually a much harder job). See the section "Programming" in Chapter 8 for a brief introduction to scripting.

- In general, text-based interfaces are much easier than GUIs for sight- and hearing-impaired users.

We aren't saying that the command-line interface is right for every situation. For instance, using the Web—with its graphics and links—is usually easier with a GUI web browser. But the command line is the fundamental way to use Unix. Understanding it will let you work on any Unix system, with or without windows.

What This Handbook Covers

This book teaches basic system utility commands to get you started with Unix. Instead of overwhelming you with lots of details, we want you to be comfortable in the Unix environment as soon as possible. So we cover a command's most useful features instead of describing all its options in detail.

We also assume that your computer works properly; someone has started it, knows the procedure for turning the power off, and knows how to perform system maintenance. In other words, we don't cover Unix system administration.

Unix users can choose between many different user interfaces—shells and window systems. Our examples show the **bash** shell and the GNOME and KDE window environments. We've chosen them because they're popular and make good examples, not because we think they're always "the best." If you do advanced work or set up Unix systems for other users, we recommend learning about a variety of shells and window systems and choosing the best ones for your needs. The principles explained in this book should help you use any Unix configuration.

What's New in the Fifth Edition

Unix keeps evolving, and this book changes with it. Although most tips in this book work on all Unix systems, old and new, there have been changes since 1997 that justify a fifth edition. Over the years, readers have asked us to include topics that couldn't be covered in just a few paragraphs—a text editor, for instance. We've decided to let this little book grow just a bit by adding several-page overviews of popular Unix tools: the Pico text editor, the Pine email program, the Lynx web browser, and two interactive chat programs. Networking is much more common, so we've added a new chapter about it. Our windowing examples show newer window systems and you'll find sections about command-line editing. There's a new Glossary with definitions of common terms, and the Index has also been expanded. Finally, we've made changes suggested by our readers.

Format

The following sections describe conventions used in this handbook.

Commands

We introduce each main concept first, and then break it into task-oriented sections. Each section shows the best command to use for a task, explains what it does, and shows the syntax (how to put the command line together). The syntax is given like this:

  rm *filename*

Commands appear in **boldface** type (in this example, **rm**). You should type the command exactly as it appears in the example. The variable parts (here, *filename*) will appear in *italic* type; you must supply your own value. To enter this command, you would type **rm** followed by a space and the name of the file that you want to remove, then press the RETURN key. (Your keyboard may have a key labeled ENTER or an arrow with a right-angle shaft instead of a RETURN key.) Throughout this book, the term *enter* means to type a command and press RETURN to run it.

Examples

Examples show what should happen as you enter a command. Some examples assume that you've created certain files. If you haven't, you may not get the results shown.

We use typewriter-style characters for examples. Items you type to try the example are **boldface**. System messages and responses are normal text.

Here's an example:

```
$ date
Tue Oct  9 13:39:24 MST 2001
$
```

The character "$" is the shell (system) prompt. To do this example, you would type **date** and then press RETURN . The **date** command responds "Tue Oct 9 13:39:24 MST 2001" and then returns you to the prompt.

Text you see in examples may not be exactly what you see on your screen. Different Unix versions have commands with different outputs. Sometimes we edit screen samples to eliminate distracting text or make them fit the page.

Problem Checklist

We've included a problem checklist in some sections. You may skip these parts and go back to them if you have a problem.

Exercises

Some sections have exercises to reinforce text you've read. Follow the exercises, but don't be afraid to experiment on your own.

Exercises have two columns. The lefthand column tells you what to do and the righthand column tells you how to do it. For example, a line in the section "Exercise: entering a few commands," near the end of Chapter 1, shows the following:

Get today's date   Enter **date**

To follow the exercise, type in the word **date** on your keyboard and then press the RETURN key. The lefthand column tells you what will happen.

After you try the commands, you'll have a better idea of the ones you want to learn more about. You can then get more information from a source in the section "Documentation," in Chapter 8.

Comments and Questions

Please address comments and questions concerning this book to the publisher:

O'Reilly & Associates, Inc.
1005 Gravenstein Highway North
Sebastopol, CA 95472
(800) 998-9938 (in the United States or Canada)
(707) 829-0515 (international or local)
(707) 829-0104 (fax)

To ask technical questions or comment on the book, send email to:

    bookquestions@oreilly.com

We have a web site for the book where examples, errata, and any plans for future editions are listed. You can access this site at:

    http://www.oreilly.com/catalog/lunix5/

For more information about books, conferences, Resource Centers, and the O'Reilly Network, see the O'Reilly web site at:

    http://www.oreilly.com

If you write to us, please include information about your Unix environment and the computer you use. You'll have our thanks, along with thanks from future readers of this handbook.

Acknowledgments

H. Milton Peek reviewed the first draft of this edition. Jeff Kawski acted as the technical editor. Chris Stone of O'Reilly & Associates, Inc. gave information about Mac OS X and reviewed the section about it. And Tim, thanks from Jerry for all your advice and support during my 12 years of writing for O'Reilly.

1

Getting Started

Before you can use Unix, a system staff person has to set up a Unix *account* for you. The account is identified by your *username*, which is usually a single word or an abbreviation. Think of this account as your office—it's your place in the Unix environment. Other users may also be at work on the same system. At many sites, there will be a whole network of Unix computers. So in addition to knowing your username, you may also need to know the *hostname* (name) of the computer that has your account. Alternatively, your account may be shared between all computers on the local network, and you may be able to log into any of them.

Once you've logged in to your account, you'll interact with your system by typing commands at a command line, to a program called a *shell*. You'll get acquainted with the shell, enter a few commands, and see how to handle common problems. To finish your Unix session, you'll log out.

Working in the Unix Environment

Each user communicates with the computer from a terminal. To get into the Unix environment, you first connect to the Unix computer. (Your terminal is probably already connected to a computer.* But Unix systems also let you log into other computers across a network. In this case, log into your local computer first, then use a remote login command to connect to the remote computer. See the section "Remote Logins" in Chapter 6.)

---

* Some terminals can connect to many computers through a kind of switchboard called a *port contender* or *data switch*. On these terminals, start by telling the port contender which computer you want to connect to.

After connecting your terminal, if needed, you start a session by logging in to your Unix account. To log in, you need your username and a *password*. Logging in does two things: it identifies which user is in a session, and it tells the computer that you're ready to start work. When you've finished, log out—and, if necessary, disconnect from the Unix computer.

---

^M If someone else has your username and password, they probably can log into your account and do anything you can. They can read private information, corrupt or delete important files, send email messages as if they came from you, and more. If your computer is connected to a network—the Internet or a local network inside your organization—intruders may also be able to log in without sitting at your keyboard! See the section "Remote Logins" in Chapter 6 for one explanation of one way this can be done.

Anyone may be able to get your username—it's usually part of your email address, for instance. Your password is what keeps others from logging in as you. Don't leave your password anywhere around your computer. Don't give your password to anyone who asks you for it unless you're sure they'll preserve your account security. Also don't send your password by email; it can be stored, unprotected, on other systems and on backup tapes, where other people may find it and then break into your account.

If you suspect that someone is using your account, ask system staff for advice. If you can't do that, setting a new password may help; see the section "Changing Your Password" in Chapter 3.

Unix systems are case sensitive. Most usernames, commands, and filenames use lowercase letters (though good passwords use a mixture of lower- and uppercase letters). Before you log in, be sure your CAPS LOCK key is off.

Connecting to the Unix Computer

If you see a message from the computer that looks something like this:

```
login:
```

you're probably connected! You can skip ahead to the section "Logging in Nongraphically" and log in.

Otherwise, if someone nearby uses the same kind of computer system you do, the easiest way to find out if you're connected is probably to ask for help. (We can't cover every user's situation exactly. There are just too many possibilities.)

If there's no one to ask, look ahead at the section "Logging in Nongraphically," later in this chapter, as well as the section "Starting X" in Chapter 2 and the section "Remote Logins" in Chapter 6. You may recognize your situation.

If that doesn't help, but your computer seems to be running an operating system other than Unix (such as Microsoft Windows), check your menus and icons for one with the name of the Unix computer you're supposed to connect to. You might also find a program named either **telnet**, **eXceed**, **ssh**, **VMware**, **procomm**, **qmodem**, **kermit**, or **minicom**, or something relating to remote access.

Logging in Nongraphically

The process of making yourself known to the computer system and getting to your Unix account is called *logging in*. If you've connected to the Unix host from another operating system, you may have been logged into Unix automatically; in this case, you should be able to run Unix programs, as shown later in this chapter in the section "Shells in a Window System" and the section "The Shell Prompt." Otherwise, before you can start work, you must connect your terminal or terminal window to the computer you need (as in the previous section) and identify yourself to the Unix system.

There are generally two ways to log in: graphically and nongraphically. If your screen has a window or windows floating in it, something like Figure 2-2A, you probably need to log in graphically, as explained by "the section "A. Ready to Run X (with a Graphical Login)" in Chapter 2.

Otherwise, to log in nongraphically, enter your username (usually your name or initials) and your private password. The password does not appear as you enter it.

When you have logged in successfully, you'll get some system messages and finally the shell prompt (where you can enter Unix commands). A successful login to the system named *nutshell* could look like Example 1-1.

Example 1-1. Nongraphical login

```
nutshell login: john
Password:
Last login: Mon Oct  8 14:34:51 EST 2001 from joe_pc
Sun Microsystems Inc.   SunOS 5.7      Generic October 1998

------------- NOTICE TO ALL USERS -----------------
The hosts nutshell, mongo, and cruncher will be down
for maintenance from 6 to 9 PM tonight.
---------------------------------------------------

My opinions may have changed, but not the fact that I am right.
Tue Oct  9 12:24:48 MST 2001
$
```

In this example, the system messages include a maintenance notice, a "fortune," and the date. Although this example doesn't show it, you may be asked for your *terminal type*, accounting or chargeback information, and so on. The last line to appear is the Unix shell prompt. When you reach this point, you're logged in to your account and can use Unix commands.

Instead of a shell prompt, you may get a menu of choices ("email," "news," and so on). If one choice is something like "shell prompt" or "command prompt," select it. Then you'll be able to follow descriptions and examples in this book.

The messages you see at login time differ from system to system and day to day. Shell prompts can also differ. Examples in this book use the currency sign $ as a prompt.

Let's summarize logging in nongraphically, step by step:

1. If needed, connect your terminal or terminal window to the Unix system.

2. Get a "login:" prompt.

3. Type in your username in *lowercase letters* at the prompt. For example, if your login name is "john," type:

   ```
   login: john
   ```

   Press the RETURN key.

   The system should prompt you to enter your password. If passwords aren't used on your system, you can skip the next step.

4. If you were assigned a password, type it at the prompt. For security,
    your password is not displayed as you type it:

    Password:

    Press the $\boxed{\text{RETURN}}$ key.

The system checks your account name and password, and if they're correct, logs you in to your account.

Problem checklist

Nothing seemed to happen after I logged in.
>   Wait a minute, since the system may just be slow. If you still get
>   nothing, ask other users if they have the same problem.

The system says "login incorrect."
>   If you have a choice of computer to log into (as we explained at the
>   start of this chapter in the section "Working in the Unix Environ-
>   ment"), check that you're connected to the right computer. If you
>   have accounts on several computers, be sure you're using the correct
>   username and password for this computer. Otherwise, try logging in
>   again, taking care to enter the username and password correctly. Be
>   sure to type your username at the "login:" prompt and your password
>   at the "password:" prompt. Backspacing may not work while entering
>   either of these; if you make a mistake, use $\boxed{\text{RETURN}}$ to get a new
>   "login:" prompt and try again. Also make sure to use the exact com-
>   bination of upper- and lowercase letters your password contains.

>   If you still fail after trying to log in a few more times, check with the
>   person who created your account to confirm your username and pass-
>   word.

All letters are in UPPERCASE and/or have backslashes (\) before them.
>   You probably entered your username in uppercase letters. Type **exit**
>   at the shell prompt and log in again.

The Unix Shell

Once you have a shell prompt, you're working with a program called a
shell. The shell interprets command lines you enter, runs programs you
ask for, and generally coordinates what happens between you and the
Unix operating system. Common shells include Bourne (**sh**), Korn (**ksh**),
and C (**csh**) shells, as well as **bash** and **tcsh**.

For a beginner, differences between shells are slight. If you plan to work a lot with Unix, though, you should learn more about your shell and its special commands.*

Shells in a Window System

If you're using a window system, as described in Chapter 2, get a shell by opening a *terminal window*—if you don't already have a terminal window open or iconified (minimized) somewhere, that is. (Figure 2-1 shows an example, but yours may look different; the important thing is that the window have a shell prompt in it.) Check your menus and icons for a command with "terminal" or "term" in its name, or a picture of a blank terminal (like a TV screen) in its icon; one common program is **xterm**.

The Shell Prompt

When the system is ready to run a command, the shell outputs a *prompt* to tell you that you can enter a command line.

Shell prompts usually end with $ or %. The prompt can be customized, though, so your own shell prompt may be different.

A prompt that ends with a hash mark (#) usually means that you're logged in as the *superuser*. The superuser doesn't have the protections for standard users that are built into the Unix system. In this case, we recommend that you stop work until you've found out how to access your personal Unix account.†

Entering a Command Line

Entering a command line at the shell prompt tells the computer what to do. Each command line includes the name of a Unix program. When you press ⌐RETURN⌐, the shell interprets your command line and executes the program.

---

* To find out which shell you're using, run the commands **echo $SHELL** and **ps $$**. (See the section "Entering a Command Line," later in this chapter.) The answer, something like *bash* or */bin/bash*, is your shell's name or pathname.

† This can happen if you're using a window system that was started by the superuser when the system was rebooted. Or maybe your prompt has been customized to end with # when you aren't the superuser.

The first word that you type at a shell prompt is always a Unix command (or program name). Like most things in Unix, program names are case sensitive; if the program name is lowercase (and most are), you must type it in lowercase. Some simple command lines have just one word, which is the program name. For more information, see the section "Syntax of Unix Command Lines," later in this chapter.

date

An example single-word command is **date**. Entering the command **date** displays the current date and time:

```
$ date
Tue Oct  9 13:39:24 MST 2001
$
```

As you type a command line, the system simply collects your keyboard input. Pressing the ⌈RETURN⌉ key tells the shell that you've finished entering text and that it can run the program.

who

Another simple command is **who**. It displays a list of each logged-on user's username, terminal number, and login time. Try it now, if you'd like.

The **who** program can also tell you who is logged in at your terminal. The command line is **who am i**. This command line consists of the command (**who**, the program's name) and arguments (**am i**). (Arguments are explained in the section "Syntax of Unix Command Lines," later in this chapter.)

```
$ who am i
cactus!john    tty23   Oct  6 08:26     (rose)
```

The response shown in this example says that:

- "I am" John (actually, my username is *john*).
- I'm logged on to the computer named "cactus."
- I'm using terminal 23.
- I logged in at 8:26 on the morning of October 6.
- I started my login from another computer named "rose."

Not all versions of **who am i** give the same information.

Recalling Previous Commands

Modern Unix shells remember command lines you've typed before. They can even remember commands from previous login sessions. This handy feature can save you a lot of retyping common commands. As with many things in Unix, though, there are several different ways to do this; we don't have room to show and explain them all. You can get more information from sources listed in the section "Documentation" in Chapter 8.

After you've typed and executed several command lines, try pressing the up-arrow key on your keyboard. If your shell is configured to understand this, you should see the previous command line after your shell prompt, just as you typed it before. Pressing the up-arrow again recalls the previous command line, and so on. Also, as you'd expect, the down-arrow key will recall more recent command lines.

To execute one of these remembered commands, just press the RETURN key. (Your cursor doesn't have to be at the end of the command line.)

Once you've recalled a command line, you can also edit it. If you don't want to execute any remembered commands, cancel the command line with CTRL-C . Next, the section "Correcting a Command Line" explains both of these.

Correcting a Command Line

What if you make a mistake in a command line? Suppose you typed **dare** instead of **date** and pressed the RETURN key before you realized your mistake. The shell will give you an error message:

```
$ dare
dare: command not found
$
```

Don't be too concerned about getting error messages. Sometimes you'll get an error even if it appears that you typed the command correctly. This can be caused by typing control characters that are invisible on the screen. Once the prompt returns, reenter your command.

As we said earlier (in the section "Recalling Previous Commands") most modern shells let you recall previous commands and edit command lines. If you'll do a lot of work at the shell prompt, it's worth learning these handy techniques. They take more time to learn than we can spend here, though—except to mention that, on those shells, the left-arrow and right-arrow keys may move your cursor along the command line to the point where you want to make a change. Here, let's concentrate on simple methods that work with all shells.

If you see a mistake before you press RETURN , you can use the *erase character* to erase and correct the mistake.

The erase character differs from system to system and from account to account, and can be customized. The most common erase characters are:

*   BACKSPACE
*   DELETE , DEL , or RUBOUT
*   CTRL-H

CTRL-H is called a *control character*. To type a control character (for example, CTRL-H), hold down the CTRL key, then press the letter "h." In the text, we will write control characters as CTRL-H , but in the examples, we will use the standard notation: ^H. This is *not* the same as pressing the ^ (caret) key, letting go, and then typing an H!

The key labeled DEL may be used as the *interrupt character* instead of the erase character. (It's labeled DELETE or RUBOUT on some terminals.) This key is used to interrupt or cancel a command, and can be used in many (but not all) cases when you want to quit what you're doing. Another character often programmed to do the same thing is CTRL-C .

Other common control characters are:

CTRL-U
> Erases the whole input line; you can start over.

CTRL-S
> Pauses output from a program that's writing to the screen. This can be confusing; we don't recommend using CTRL-S , but want you to be aware of it.

CTRL-Q
> Restarts output after a pause by CTRL-S .

CTRL-D
> Used to signal end-of-input for some programs (such as **cat** and **mail**, explained in Chapter 5 and Chapter 6) and return you to a shell prompt. If you type CTRL-D at a shell prompt, it may close your terminal window or log you out of the Unix system.

Find the erase and interrupt characters for your account and write them here:

_____ Backspace and erase a character

_____ Interrupt a program

Logging Out

To end a Unix session, you must log out. You should *not* end a session by just turning off your terminal!

If you're using a window system, first close open windows and then close the window system; see the section "Quitting" in Chapter 2 for more information. If you logged in graphically, that should end your login session. But, if you logged in nongraphically before you started the window system, closing the window system should take you back to a shell prompt (where you originally typed **xinit** or **startx**). In that case, use the following steps to finish logging out.

If you aren't currently using a window system, you can log out by entering the command **exit** at a shell prompt. (In many cases, the command **logout** will also work.) Depending on your shell, you may also be able to log out simply by typing CTRL-D .

What happens next depends on the place from which you've logged in: if your terminal is connected directly to the computer, the "login:" prompt should appear on the screen. Otherwise, if you were connected to a remote computer, the shell prompt from your local computer should reappear on your screen. (That is, you're still logged in to your local computer.) Repeat the process if you want to log out from the local computer.

After you've logged out, you can turn off your terminal or leave it on for the next user. But, if the power switch for your terminal is the same as the power switch for the whole Unix computer system, do *not* simply turn off that power switch! Ask a local expert for help with shutting down your Unix system safely.

Problem checklist

The first few times you use Unix, you aren't likely to have the following problems. But you may encounter these problems later, as you do more advanced work.

You get another shell prompt or the shell says "logout: not login shell"

You've been using a subshell (a shell created by your original login shell). To end each subshell, type **exit** (or just type ⌞CTRL-D⌟) until you're logged out.

The shell says "There are stopped jobs" or "There are running jobs."

Many Unix systems have a feature called *job control* that lets you suspend a program temporarily while it's running or keep it running separately in the "background." One or more programs you ran during your session has not ended, but is stopped (paused) or in the background. Enter **fg** to bring each stopped job into the foreground, then quit the program normally. (See Chapter 7 for more information.)

Syntax of Unix Command Lines

Unix command lines can be simple, one-word entries such as the **date** command. They can also be more complex; you may need to type more than the command or program name.*

A Unix command may or may not have *arguments*. An argument can be an option or a filename. The general format for Unix command lines is:

command *option(s) filename(s)*

There isn't a single set of rules for writing Unix commands and arguments, but you can use these general rules in most cases:

- Enter commands in lowercase.

- *Options* modify the way in which a command works. Options are often single letters prefixed with a dash (-, also called "hyphen" or "minus") and set off by any number of spaces or tabs. Multiple options in one command line can be set off individually (such as **-a -b**). In some cases, you can combine them after a single dash (such as **-ab**)—but most commands' documentation doesn't tell you whether this will work; you'll have to try it.

  Some commands, including those on Linux systems, also have options made from complete words or phrases and starting with two dashes, like **--delete** or **--confirm-delete**. When you enter a command line, you can use this option style, the single-letter options (which all start with a single dash), or both.

---

* The command can be the name of a Unix program (such as **date**), or it can be a command that's built into the shell (such as **exit**). You probably don't need to worry about this! You can read more precise definitions of these terms and others in Glossary.

- The argument *filename* is the name of a file that you want to use. Most Unix programs also accept multiple filenames, separated by spaces. If you don't enter a filename correctly, you may get a response such as "*filename*: no such file or directory" or "*filename*: cannot open."

  Some commands, such as **telnet** and **who** (shown earlier in this chapter), have arguments that aren't filenames.

- You must type spaces between commands, options, and filenames.

- Options come before filenames.

  In a few cases, an option has another argument associated with it; type this special argument just after its option. Most options don't work this way, but you should know about them. The **sort** command is an example of this: you can tell **sort** to write the sorted text to a filename given after its -o option. In the following example, **sort** reads the file *sortme* (given as an argument), and writes to the file *sorted* (given after the -o option):

  ```
  $ sort -o sorted -n sortme
  ```

  We also used the -n option in that example. But -n is a more standard option; it has nothing to do with the final argument *sortme* on that command line. So, we also could have written the command line this way:

  ```
  $ sort -n -o sorted sortme
  ```

  Another example is the **mail** -s option, shown in the section "Sending Mail from a Shell Prompt" of Chapter 6. Don't be too concerned about these special cases, though. If a command needs an option like this, its documentation will say so.

- Command lines can have other special characters, some of which we see later in this book. They also can have several separate commands. For instance, you can write two or more commands on the same command line, each separated by a semicolon (;). Commands entered this way are executed one after another by the shell.

Unix has a lot of commands! Don't try to memorize all of them. In fact, you'll probably need to know just a few commands and their options. As time goes on, you'll learn these commands and the best way to use them for your job. We cover some useful Unix commands in later chapters. This book's quick reference card has quick reminders.

Let's look at a sample Unix command. The **ls** program displays a list of files. You can use it with or without options and arguments. If you enter:

    $ **ls**

you'll see a list of filenames. But if you enter:

    $ **ls -l**

there'll be an entire line of information for each file. The –l option (a dash and a lowercase letter "L") changes the normal **ls** output to a long format. You can also get information about a particular file by using its name as the second argument. For example, to find out about a file called *chap1*, enter:

    $ **ls -l chap1**

Many Unix commands have more than one option. For instance, **ls** has the –a (*all*) option for listing hidden files. You can use multiple options in either of these ways:

    $ **ls -a -l**
    $ **ls -al**

You must type one space between the command name and the dash that introduces the options. If you enter **ls-al**, the shell will say "ls–al: command not found."

Exercise: entering a few commands

The best way to get used to Unix is to enter some commands. To run a command, type the command and then press the ⌐RETURN¬ key. Remember that almost all Unix commands are typed in lowercase.

Get today's date.	Enter **date**
List logged-in users.	Enter **who**
Obtain more information about users.	Enter **who -u** or **finger** or **w**
Find out who is at your terminal.	Enter **who am i**
Enter two commands in the same line.	Enter **who am i;date**
Mistype a command.	Enter **woh**

In this session, you've tried several simple commands and seen the results on the screen.

Types of Commands

When you use a program, you'll want to know how to control it. How can you tell it what job you want done? Do you give instructions before the program starts, or after it's started? There are three general ways to give commands on a Unix system, three different kinds of programs. It's good to be aware of them.

1. Some Unix programs work only with a window system. For instance, when you type **netscape** at a shell prompt (or click a button or choose the command from a menu), the Netscape web browser starts. It opens one or more windows on your screen. The program has its own way to receive your commands—through menus and buttons on its windows, for instance.

2. You've also seen (previously, in the section "Syntax of Unix Command Lines") Unix commands that you enter at a shell prompt. These programs work in a window system (from a terminal window) or from any terminal. Control those programs from the Unix command line— that is, by typing options and arguments from a shell prompt before you start the program running. After you start the program, wait for it to finish; you generally don't interact with it.

3. Some Unix programs that work in terminals have commands of their own. (If you'd like some examples, see the section "Looking Inside Files with less" in Chapter 3 and the section "The Pico Text Editor" in Chapter 4.) These programs may accept options and arguments on their command line. But, once you start the program, it prints its own prompt and/or menus and it understands its own commands; it takes instructions from your keyboard, which weren't given on its command line.

    For instance, if you enter **pine** at a shell prompt, you'll see a new prompt from the **pine** program. Enter Pine commands to handle email messages. When you enter the special command **q** to quit the **pine** program, **pine** will stop prompting you. Then you'll get another shell prompt, where you can enter other Unix commands.

The Unresponsive Terminal

During your Unix session (while you're logged in), your terminal may not respond when you type a command, or the display on your screen may stop at an unusual place. That's called a "hung" or "frozen" terminal or session.

(Note that most of the techniques in this section apply to terminal windows in a window system, but not to nonterminal windows such as a web browser. In Chapter 2, the section "Unresponsive Windows" should help with windows in general.)

A session can hang for several reasons. For instance, the connection between your terminal and the computer can get too busy; your terminal has to wait its turn. (Other users or computers probably share the same connection.) In that case, your session starts by itself in a few moments. You should *not* try to "un-hang" the session by entering extra commands because those commands will all take effect after the connection resumes.

If the system doesn't respond for quite a while (how long that is depends on your individual situation; ask other users about their experiences), the following solutions usually work. Try the following steps in the order shown until the system responds:

1. Press the RETURN key *once*.

    You may have typed text at a prompt (for example, a command line at a shell prompt) but haven't yet pressed RETURN to say that you're done typing and your text should be interpreted.

2. If you can type commands, but nothing happens when you press RETURN, try pressing LINEFEED or typing CTRL-J. If this works, your terminal needs resetting to fix the RETURN key. Some systems have a **reset** command that you can run by typing CTRL-J **reset** CTRL-J. If this doesn't work, you may need to log out and log back in or turn your terminal off and on again. (But, before you turn off your terminal, read the notes earlier and later in this chapter about turning off the power.)

3. If your shell has job control (see Chapter 7), type CTRL-Z.

    This suspends a program that may be running and gives you another shell prompt. Now you can enter the **jobs** command to find the program's name, then restart the program with **fg** or terminate it with **kill**.

4. Use your interrupt key (found earlier in this chapter in the section "Correcting a Command Line"—typically DELETE or CTRL-C).

    This interrupts a program that may be running. (Unless a program is run in the background, as described in the section "Running a Command in the Background" in Chapter 7, the shell waits for it to finish before giving a new prompt. A long-running program may thus appear to hang the terminal.) If this doesn't work the first time, try it once more; doing it more than twice usually won't help.

5.   Type CTRL-Q .

     If output has been stopped with CTRL-S , this will restart it. (Note
     that some systems will automatically issue CTRL-S if they need to
     pause output; this character may not have been typed from the key-
     board.)

6.   Check that the NO SCROLL key (if you have one) is not locked or
     toggled on.

     This key stops the screen display from scrolling upward. If your key-
     board has a NO SCROLL key that can be toggled on and off by press-
     ing it over and over, keep track of how many times you've pressed it
     as you try to free yourself. If it doesn't seem to help, be sure you've
     pressed it an even number of times; this leaves the key in the same
     state it was when you started.

7.   Check the physical connection from the terminal to the system.

8.   Type CTRL-D *once* at the beginning of a new line.

     Some programs (such as **mail**) expect text from the user. A program
     may be waiting for an end-of-input character from you to tell it that
     you've finished entering text. Typing CTRL-D may cause you to log
     out, so you should try this only as a last resort.

9.   If you're using a window system, close (terminate) the window you're
     using and open a new one. See the section "Unresponsive Windows"
     in Chapter 2.

     Otherwise, turn your terminal off, wait ten seconds or so, then turn it
     on again. This may also log you out, but it may not; your old login
     session could still be running. You can check for old processes and
     terminate them (as explained in Chapter 7 in the section "Checking on
     a Process" and in the section "Cancelling a Process")—although this
     isn't an easy thing for a beginner to do, so you might want help.

2

Using Window Systems

All versions of Unix work with alphanumeric terminals that handle a single session in a single screen, such as those described in Chapter 1. On most modern Unix versions, you can also use a *window system*. A window system is software that lets a single screen handle many sessions at once.* Window systems use a mouse or another device (such as a trackball) to move a *pointer* across the screen. The pointer can be used to select and move parts of the screen, copy and paste text, work with menus of commands, and more. If you've used a Macintosh or Microsoft Windows, among others, you've used a window system. Figure 2-1 shows a typical screen with windows.

This chapter introduces the X Window System, which is called X for short, the most common Unix window system. This introduction should also help you use window systems other than X. •

---

* If you're using a PC operating system, such as Linux or NetBSD, your system probably also supports *virtual consoles*. See the Glossary for a definition and more information.

Introduction to Windowing

Like Unix, X is very flexible. The appearance of windows, the way menus and icons work, as well as other features, are controlled by a program called the *window manager*. There are many different window managers; some have many features and "eye candy," while others are simple and have just basic features. A window manager can make your desktop look a lot like a Macintosh or Microsoft Windows system, or it can look completely different. Your system may also have an optional *desktop environment* that provides even more features, such as support for "drag and drop" (for example, printing a file by dragging its icon onto a printer icon). Two popular desktop environments are GNOME and KDE. In this chapter, we show GNOME with the Sawfish window manager, as well as KDE with the kwm window manager. Details of other window managers, including how they make your screen look, are somewhat different—but this chapter should help you use them, too.

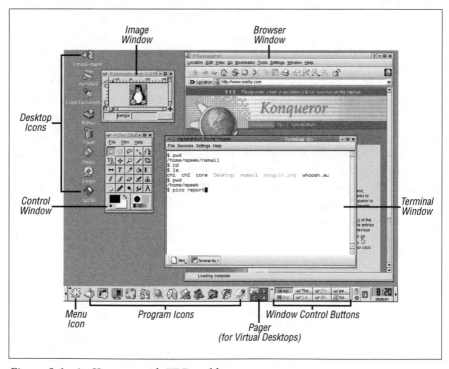

Figure 2-1. An X screen with KDE and kwm

Starting X

There are several ways to start X and its window manager. This section explains a few common ways. Figure 2-2 shows some steps along a few different paths to starting X. (The large "X" on the figures is the mouse pointer, or cursor, that you may see on your screen.) If your screen is like any of the following, refer to the section noted. If none fits your situation, skim through the next three sections or ask another X user for help.

- Figure 2-2A, **xdm** (or another program, such as **gdm** or **kdm**) is running and waiting for you to log in graphically. Start reading at Section A.

- Figure 2-2B has a standard Unix login session; the X Window System is not running. Start reading at Section B.

- Figure 2-2C shows X running, but a window manager probably isn't. (You can tell because the window doesn't have a *frame* around it: there's no titlebar or border.) Read Section C.

- Figure 2-2D shows the window with a frame (titlebar and border), so X and the window manager (in this example, **mwm**) are running. You're ready to go! Skip ahead to the section "Running Programs."

A. Ready to Run X (with a Graphical Login)

Some terminals, like the one whose screen is shown in Figure 2-2A, are ready to use X. Your terminal has probably been set up to use one of the X display managers called **xdm**, **gdm**, **kdm**, or others; these log you in to your account and usually also start the window manager.

When you start, there's a single window in the middle of the screen that has two prompts like "login:" and "password:". The cursor sits to the right of the "login:" line. To log in, type your username (login name) and press RETURN , then do the same for your password. The login window disappears.

If a screen something like Figure 2-1 or Figure 2-2D appears, you're ready to use X. You can skip ahead to "the section "Running Programs."

If you get a screen such as Figure 2-2C (a single window with no title and no border), read Section C. Or, if you get a blank screen, press and release your mouse buttons one by one, slowly, to see if a menu pops up.

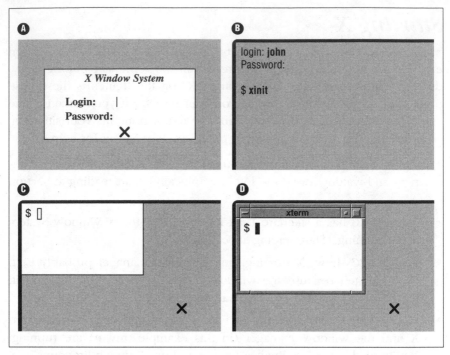

Figure 2-2. Four scenarios that may occur while starting X

B. Starting X from a Standard Unix Session

If your terminal shows something like Figure 2-2B, with a standard Unix "login:" prompt (not in a separate window; the display fills the whole screen, making it look like a terminal), X isn't running. Log in (as the section "Logging in Nongraphically" in Chapter 1 explains) and get a shell prompt (such as $ or %). Next, you need to start X. Try this command first:

```
$ startx
```

If that doesn't seem to work (after waiting a minute or so; X can be slow to start), try the command **xinit** instead. If all goes well, your screen sprouts at least one window. If the window looks like Figure 2-2C, without a titlebar or border from a window manager, read Section C. Otherwise, your window manager is running, so skip ahead to the section "Running Programs."

Problem checklist

No windows open. I get the message "Fatal server error: No screens found."
Your terminal may not be able to run X. Try another terminal or ask a local expert.

C. Starting the Window Manager

Once you have a window open with a shell prompt in it (usually $ or %), you can start the window manager program. If a window manager isn't running, windows won't have frames (with titles, control boxes, and so on). Also, if you move the pointer outside any window (to the desktop) and press the mouse buttons, menus won't appear unless the window manager is running. If you have to start the window manager by hand, your account probably hasn't been set up correctly. To make your life easier, get help from an X-pert and fix your account!

If you need to start the window manager by hand, move your pointer into the terminal window. At the shell prompt, type the name of your window manager, followed by an ampersand (&). If you don't know your window manager's name, try the following names, one by one, until one works (i.e., doesn't give you a "command not found" error): **gnome-session**, **startkde**, **wmaker**, **afterstep**, **fvwm2**, **fvwm**, or **twm**. For example:

```
$ fvwm &
[1] 12345
$
```

In a few moments, the window should have a frame. (For more about starting programs, see the section "Terminal Windows," later in this chapter.)

Running Programs

A window manager can open windows of its own. But the main use of a window manager is to manage windows opened by other programs. We mention a few window programs here; the section "Other X Window Programs," near the end of this chapter, has more.

One of the most important X features is that windows can come either from programs running on your local computer, or over a network from programs running on remote computers. The remote computers can run Unix or another operating system. So, if your favorite program from another operating system doesn't run under Unix but has an X interface, you may be able to run that program on its native OS and display its windows with X on your Unix computer. (Check your program's documentation; see the section "Documentation" in Chapter 8.) Researchers can run graphical data analysis programs on supercomputers in other parts of the country and see the results in their offices. There's much more than we can explain here. We cover the basics here and in Chapter 6 in the section "Windows from Other Computers," which also has a figure showing how this works. If you'll do a lot of work with X, you may want a detailed reference that explains X and your window manager.

Setting Focus

Of all the windows on your screen, only one window receives the keystrokes you type. This window is usually highlighted in some way. For instance, the titlebar of the window that receives your input may be blue instead of the default grey color. In X jargon, choosing the window you type to is called "setting the *input focus*." Most window managers can be configured to set the focus in one of the following ways:

- Move the mouse pointer into a window and click a mouse button (usually the first button; see the section "Working with a Mouse," later in this chapter). In some systems, you may need to click on the titlebar at the top of the window.

- Simply move the pointer inside a window.

Your window manager may be configured to give the input focus automatically to any new windows that pop up.

Terminal Windows

One of the most important windows is a *terminal window*. A terminal window has a Unix session inside with a shell prompt, just like a miniature alphanumeric terminal. You can have several terminal windows running at the same time, each doing something different. To enter a Unix command or answer a prompt in a window, set the focus there and type. Programs in other windows will keep running; if they need input from you, they'll wait just as they would on a standard terminal.

Quite a few programs make terminal windows. One of the best-known programs is **xterm**. Others include GNOME Terminal and **konsole**. All perform the same basic job: they allow you to interact with Unix from a shell prompt.

Figure 2-2D and Figure 2-4 show a single terminal window with a shell prompt ($). If you enter a Unix command (such as **date**) at the prompt, it runs just as it would on a terminal that isn't under the X Window System.

You can also start other X-based window programs (sometimes called *X clients*) by entering the program's name at a shell prompt in any terminal window. Although you can start new programs (such as terminal windows, **xcalc**, and so on) from any open terminal window on your computer, we recommend starting them all from the first terminal window that you open. If you do that, and if your shell has job control (see Chapter 7), it's easy to find and control all the other programs and their windows.

Here's an example. To start the calculator called **xcalc**, enter this command from a terminal window:

```
$ xcalc &
[1] 12345
$
```

The shell will put the process in the background—so you get another shell prompt right away—and will print a process ID (PID) number, such as 12345. (Chapter 7 has more information on this subject.) If you forget to add the ampersand (&) at the end of the line, then kill (terminate) the **xcalc** program from the terminal window where you started it by typing your interrupt character (such as CTRL-C). You should get another shell prompt, where you can re-enter the **xcalc** command correctly.

The new window may be placed and get the focus automatically. Or, the window (or an outline of it) may "float" above the screen, following the pointer, until you point somewhere and click the first mouse button to place the window.

You can also start a new terminal window from an existing one. Just enter the program's name and an ampersand (for example, **xterm &**) at the shell prompt. Don't forget the ampersand.

The same method will start other X programs. (Later in this chapter, the section "Other X Window Programs" lists some standard X programs.)

Window Manager Menus

Your window manager probably has one or more menus, buttons, and dialogs of its own. These let you control the way the window manager works, overall. They may also launch programs, open the help system, and do other useful things that don't apply to all programs and windows that are currently open (things you can't do with an individual program's own menus, that is). For instance, a window manager menu might let you set how many rows of program launching buttons are in the panel or the color of the frame around each window.

Different window managers have different ways to do these things. To find the menus on your window manager, read its documentation or experiment a bit. You might also find that pressing different mouse buttons will open different menus. You may need to hold down the button to keep a menu visible. Move your mouse pointer around to places shown in the following, then try your mouse buttons:

- The desktop (outside any of your open windows)

- An icon with a logo—for example, the KDE gear with a K over it or the GNOME footprint

- A blank part of some standard feature of your desktop—for instance, an empty part of the panel

- Any little feature that doesn't seem to apply to a particular program (that isn't a program icon and doesn't have the title of a program or open window)—for instance, the small triangle to the right of the pager shown in Figure 2-1

You probably can add commands to some menus, or more icons to a group of program-launching icons. You might add window manager operations or commands to open other windows. For example, a "New Window" menu item can open a new terminal window for you. A "Calculator" item could start **xcalc**. Different window managers have different ways to do this. Check your documentation. To add a command, you'll need to specify either the program name (such as **xterm** or **mozilla**) or the absolute pathname of its executable file (such as */usr/X11R6/bin/xterm*). The absolute pathname varies system-to-system; you might find it using the command **which** or **type** from a shell prompt, like this:

```
$ type xterm
xterm is /usr/X11R6/bin/xterm
$ which xterm
/usr/X11R6/bin/xterm
```

Exercise: exploring your window system

Change to your home directory.	Enter **cd**.
Open two terminal windows.	Enter the program name and an ampersand (such as **xterm &**) twice, or select that item twice on a window manager menu.
Practice setting focus on both new windows and entering Unix commands in each.	Click on a window and/or move the pointer there. Enter **who am i**, etc.
Start a clock from one terminal window.	Enter **xclock &** or **oclock &**.
Start a calculator from one window and try it.	Enter **xcalc &**.
Change the working directory (see the section "Changing Your Working Directory" in Chapter 3) in only *one* terminal window.	Enter **cd /bin**.
Check the working directory in *both* terminal windows.	Enter **pwd** in both windows.
Terminate **xcalc**.	Set the focus on the **xcalc**, and either type your interrupt character (such as CTRL-C) or click the close-box (often an X in the top-right corner of the window frame).

Problem checklist

When I try to start a window program, I see "connection refused by server" or "client is not authorized to connect to server."

You may need to run a command like **xhost** or **xauth**. These commands have security implications that we can't cover adequately in this little book, though, so please check with your system staff.

When I try to start a window program, I see "Error: Can't open display."

Your DISPLAY environment variable may not be set correctly or you may need to use the **–display** option. Ask for help or check X Window System documentation.

Why are the columns of text in my terminal window jagged?

- Some programs, such as **ls –l** and **who**, expect your display to use a *fixed-width* font, where every character is the same width. If your set your terminal window to a variable-width font, the columns won't line up correctly. We recommend fixed-width fonts, such as Courier, for terminal windows.

- Your terminal mode may be incorrect. (This can happen if a program fails or is interrupted.) From a shell prompt, use the **reset** command, as explained in the section "The Unresponsive Terminal" in Chapter 1.

Working with a Mouse

Let's look at basics of using a mouse or other pointing device. We assume that your mouse has three buttons, as mice on Unix systems usually do. (If your mouse has two buttons, you may be able to simulate the missing middle button by pressing *both* of the other buttons at once. Your X system may need to be reconfigured to work this way, though.) When we say "the first button," we mean the leftmost button for right-handed users, or the rightmost button for left-handed users. (Under X, a mouse can be set for either left-handed or right-handed users, so the button you use to click on and drag is the button under your index finger.)

Pointer Shape

As you move the mouse pointer* from the desktop on to other windows or menus, the shape of the pointer changes. For instance, on some window systems, while the pointer is over the desktop, it's shaped like a big X. The pointer may change to an hourglass shape to tell you to wait. When you resize a window, the pointer could change to a cross with arrows.

Using a Mouse with xterm Windows

One advantage terminal windows have over plain (nonwindowing) terminals is you can copy and paste text within an **xterm** window or between **xterm** windows.

Although this section is specifically about **xterm** windows, most tips here also apply to other kinds of terminal windows. Check your documentation or just try these and see!

---

* The correct word for this symbol is *cursor*. But **xterm** and some other windows also have separate cursors to show where text will be entered. To avoid confusion, we use the word "pointer" for the cursor that moves all across the screen under control of the mouse.

To get started, move the pointer inside an **xterm** window and be sure it has the focus (if your window manager doesn't do that automatically). Notice that the pointer changes to an "I-beam" shape as you move it into the window. We discuss this I-beam pointer later in this section. There's also a block cursor (which is shown in all terminal windows in this chapter—and labeled at Figure 2-4.) The block cursor is the window's *insertion point*, where text goes when you type on the keyboard. The block cursor doesn't follow the mouse.

If your window doesn't have some previously completed command lines, as in Figure 2-3, type command lines at a couple of prompts; this gives you text to copy. (The **mail** command, shown in Figure 2-3 and explained in Chapter 6, is a good example, but you can use any command line that you want to rerun from another window.)

The I-beam pointer selects text for copying. Let's try it. Point to the first character of a command line (not the prompt) and click the first mouse button. Next, move the pointer to the end of the text you want to select and click the third button. The text between the first and third clicks should be highlighted; your **xterm** window should look something like Figure 2-3. (Problems? If you select the wrong text, you can undo the selection by clicking the first button anywhere in the window. If you accidentally click the second button, this may paste some random text at the block cursor; in that case, you can erase the pasted text with your backspace key.)

Another way to select text is by pointing to the first character you want to copy, then holding down the first mouse button while you drag the pointer across the text. By the time you release the mouse button, the whole area of text should be highlighted.

The instant you highlight text (as you did a moment ago), the text is also automatically copied, so you can paste it somewhere else. (In an original **xterm** window, there's no menu with a "Copy" command on it. In most X window programs—the original X programs, at least—highlighting text copies it automatically.)

You can paste text in the window you copied it from or in another window. Let's choose another open terminal window. With the block cursor at a shell prompt, click the middle mouse button *anywhere* in the window. (You *don't* have to click at the block cursor!) The selected text will be inserted (pasted) into the window at the block cursor, just as if you had typed it in. Press RETURN to run the command; otherwise, backspace over it to get back to the prompt.

You can also select text in a window just by clicking. Point to a word and double-click the first button; the word should be highlighted. Next, let's select an entire line. Point to any character on a line (a space is OK too) and triple-click the first button to highlight the whole line.

You can select and copy any text, not just command lines. With the **mail** command, for instance, you can copy a line from the body of the email message.

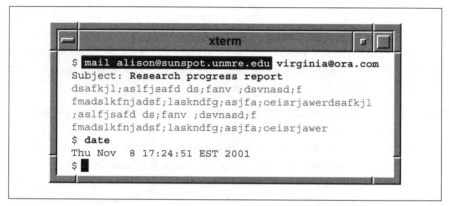

Figure 2-3. Copying a command line

The same copying and pasting works between **xterm** windows and between many other (but not all) windows that handle text. Before you paste text into an **xterm** window, always be sure the block cursor is at the place you want to insert the newly pasted text!

Problem checklist

When I try to paste text into a terminal window, it doesn't appear where I want it.

One common mistake is clicking the mouse at a particular point in the terminal window and expecting the text to be pasted there. In most terminal-based Unix applications, you need to move the insertion point (typically, a block-shaped cursor) using keyboard commands or the arrow keys. Before you paste, be sure that the insertion point is at the place you want it.

I've copied text from one window, but it won't appear when I paste it.

Unfortunately, there are several possible causes, including the following list:

- Be sure you're pressing the second (middle) mouse button to paste. If you have a two-button mouse, pressing both buttons (to act like the missing middle button) can be tough: it takes precise timing.

- Some things can erase the clipboard where your text was copied—for instance, opening certain kinds of new windows. Try copying the text again, then pasting it right away.

- The window system actually has many clipboards, and some programs don't check all clipboards to find your copied text. You may be able to paste the text into another window (such as a window-based text editor), then copy the text again and paste it where you want it.

- Some programs will let you highlight text, but the text actually isn't copied and/or pasted unless you use the "Copy" and/or "Paste" commands on the program's menu.

Can you save some or all of the text you want to copy into a temporary file? If so, you may be able to open that file in another type of window (such as a text editor), then copy from that new window. Also try using a text editor to put just the text you want into the temporary file, then read that file into the program where you originally wanted to paste the text.

Working with Windows

A window manager program helps you control windows. Various window managers do the same kinds of things, with some variation. Let's start by looking at Figure 2-4, which shows a typical window under KDE and **kwm**.

The edges of the window can be used to resize the window. The top of every window has a titlebar that includes the window title as well as three buttons.

Using the Titlebar

The titlebar is the top of a window; it has the window's title, and, usually, some buttons or other features. See Figure 2-4.

The three buttons at the top right corner have boxes inside them.

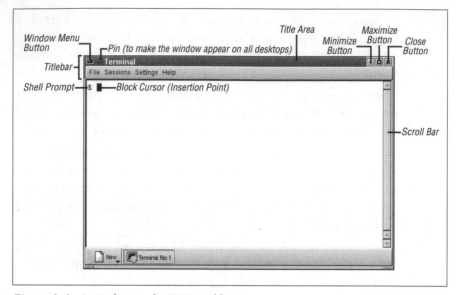

Figure 2-4. A window under KDE and kwm

- Click the button with the small square to *mimimize* the window (make the window as small as possible); this is also called "hiding" the window. With some window manager configurations, a minimized window turns into an *icon*; on others, the window may have a title button in a list of window buttons at the bottom of a window (or elsewhere). No matter how your window manager treats a minimized window, though, the important point here is that minimizing puts unneeded windows out of the way without quitting the program inside them; it also keeps you from accidentally typing into a window.

  You can restore ("show") a minimized ("hidden") window by clicking on its icon, its button on the panel at the bottom of the screen, or in several other ways—again, depending on your window manager.

- *Maximizing* a window makes it as big as the program will allow, often as big as the screen. One way to do this—which is different in different window managers, of course—is to click the button on the window frame that has a large square.

  Maximizing windows that have graphical applications in them—such as a web browser—works just fine. But it can be a bad idea to maximize terminal windows (and give them more than 80 characters per line), especially if there's a program running in that window. See the note in the section "Resizing Windows," later in this chapter.

- Clicking the box with a big "X" *kills* a window. In some window managers, clicking with the third mouse button is a more emphatic kill. (Later in this chapter, the section "Unresponsive Windows" describes this in more detail.)

It's not always a good idea to click the "X" box on a window frame—especially on a terminal window with a program running inside. Although it may seem to work (because the window closes), the programs running inside the window may not have time to finish their work and exit gracefully.

It's safer to use the program's own "exit" command. For instance, if you're running the Pico editor in a terminal window, use its CTRL-X command. If you have a shell prompt, type **exit** or press CTRL-D ; if the program has a menu or button with which to quit, use it. If there's no other choice, though, you're probably safe to click the "X" box on the frame.

The left button opens the window menu; this is explained in "the section "The Window Menu" later in this chapter.

Moving Windows and Icons

To move a window, start by pointing to the titlebar. Hold down the first mouse button and drag to the new location—then let go of the button.

Resizing Windows

If you have the pointer inside a window and then move the pointer to an edge, the pointer will probably change to another shape—an arrow, for example. If you point to a corner, you may be able to resize both sides that meet at the corner. To resize when you have the arrow pointer, press and hold (typically) the first button, then drag the window border until the window size is what you want and release the button. If you don't get quite the size you want, just do it again.

If you're using a terminal window (such as **xterm**), and a program is already running in that window (not just a shell prompt), note that resizing the window may confuse the programs currently running in it! It's best to set the terminal window size *before* you run a program.

Also, remember that standard terminals are 80 characters wide. If you're editing text in a window with a width that isn't 80 characters, it can cause trouble later when the file is viewed on a standard terminal.

Stacking Windows

You can have many windows open at once. To get some or all out of the way, minimize them. Sometimes, though, you'll want several overlapping windows on your screen:

- You could log onto the Internet, go to your favorite news website and open ten windows, each with an article you want to read. Then log off the Internet (to free your phone line) and read each window. In that case, it might be easiest to have the ten windows in a stack, and close each window after you're done—instead of minimizing all windows at the start and restoring them, one by one, as you read them.

- You might need several windows visible at the same time—for instance, reading email messages in one window while you edit a presentation in another window, with a web browser open to a company information page in a third window. You may not need to shrink windows to keep them from overlapping. Instead, windows can partly overlap, covering areas of other windows that you don't need to see.

  In X, a window doesn't always need to be on top of the stack to get the input focus (so you can type into it). If you've configured your window manager so the window with the mouse pointer over it gets the focus automatically (without clicking on the window), you can type in a window without raising it to the top of the stack. This is a handy feature of most X window managers.

To bring a window to the top, you can generally either click on its title bar with the first mouse button or use the window manager's "raise window" command. That "raise window" command is usually either on the window menu (see the following section), on a window manager menu (choose "raise window," then click on the window you want to raise), or it might be found by clicking on the window frame with the third mouse button. In the same way, your window manager probably has a "lower window" command that moves a window behind the windows it overlaps.

The Window Menu

Many window managers let you control each window by its own *window menu*. There are lots of ways to get a window menu. Here are two: click on the menu button at the top left corner of a frame (as in Figure 2-4, for KDE and the **kwm** window manager), or click on an icon (for the **mwm** window manager). Figure 2-5 shows a window menu from the Sawfish window manager. When the menu pops up, you can point to an item and click it.

Let's look at some of the Sawfish window menu operations:

- The **Minimize** and **Maximize** operations are explained in "Using the Titlebar," earlier in this chapter.

- **Close** terminates the window and the program in it. Use this as a last resort. If the program has a separate menu or quit command (for example, entering **exit** at a shell prompt in a terminal window), use it instead of **Close**. (See "Quitting," later in this chapter, for an explanation.)

- **Send window to** lets you move a window to another virtual desktop. When you point to this item, a submenu appears with a list of desktops where the window can be moved.

- **Stacking** opens a submenu that lets you control this window's position in a stack of windows.

- **History** opens a submenu that tells the window manager how to handle this particular type of window in the future. For example, the window menu in Figure 2-5 happens to be on a GNOME Terminal window. If you have the GNOME Terminal window at a particular spot near the lower-left corner of the desktop, and you choose the **Remember position** entry on this submenu, then the next GNOME Terminal window you open will open at the same place on the desktop. (Once a window has opened in this particular spot, you can always move it somewhere else.) The **Forget saved state** entry tells the window manager to forget all of the History settings you've made for this type of window.

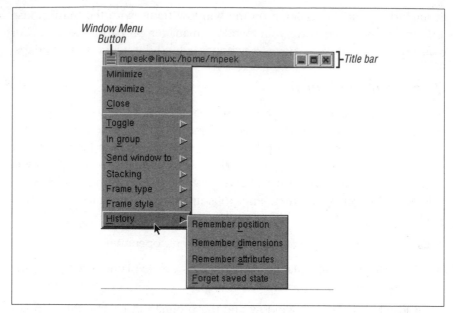

Figure 2-5. A Sawfish window menu

On the **mwm** menu (not shown here), a *keyboard shortcut* follows each command. Other window managers may have keyboard shortcuts but not list them on the menu (they could be listed on a configuration menu somewhere else). With a shortcut, you don't have to use the mouse to choose commands; you can handle window operations without taking your hands off the keyboard. For example, next to the **Minimize** entry is the shortcut hint "Alt+F9", which means that you can minimize this window without a mouse by holding down the ALT (or META) key and pressing the F9 key. Holding the SHIFT key and pressing the ESC key brings up an **mwm** window menu (and takes it away). If your keyboard doesn't have all of those keys, the menu can probably be customized to use others. Other window managers may have different keyboard shortcuts—or none at all.

Exercise

If you don't have two terminal windows open from the previous exercise, please start by opening them.

Copy and paste part of a command line.	Type **who am i;date** and press RETURN in one terminal window. Highlight the **who am i**, set focus to the other terminal window, paste the command there, and run it.
Move a window.	Grab and drag the window by its title-bar.
Iconify a window from the titlebar.	Use the Mimimize button.
Restore (de-iconify) the window.	Find the window's **Restore** command.

Other Window Manager Features

Your window manager and/or desktop environment may have some other handy features. Let's look at two. Explore these after you've learned more basic operations; they can be real timesavers!

Panel

A *panel* is a thin bar across the top or bottom of the screen. If you have a panel, it probably has icons you can click to launch a program. It also may have a row of buttons, one for each window that's either open or minimized (or both); you can use these buttons to open a minimized window or raise an open window to the top of a stack. If you move the mouse pointer over an object without clicking, a "tool tip" box may appear with more information about it. You also can try clicking on these and/or holding down your mouse buttons (try each mouse button, in turn) to see what they might do.

Pagers and Virtual Desktops

Sophisticated window managers can manage multiple desktops on the same physical screen. A *pager* lets you choose between these *virtual desktops*. Each virtual desktop is like the desktop you see when you open the window system—but you can open different windows on each virtual desktop. It's kind of like having two or more separate physical terminals stacked on top of each other, as well as side-to-side, on your desk—each with its own desktop displayed, all driven from the same keyboard and mouse. All virtual desktops appear on the same screen, but only one is visible at a time. If you're using GNOME or KDE, you may have four virtual desktops available automatically, though that number can be changed.

Think of these desktops arranged in a grid, as Figure 2-6 shows. You can refer to the desktops by saying "the desktop above" or "the desktop to the right"; they may also be numbered. The window manager has commands to let you move a window from one desktop to another (see the section "The Window Menu," earlier in this chapter). You also may be able to use the mouse to drag a window "off the edge" of one desktop and onto the next.

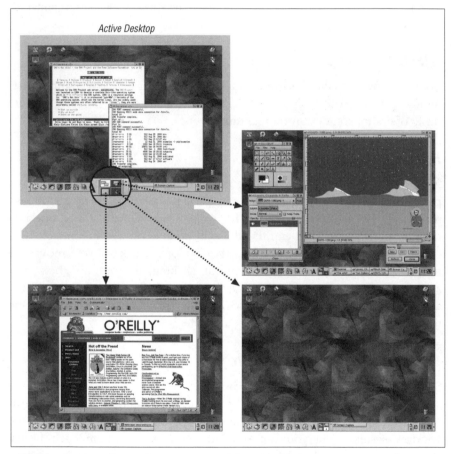

Figure 2-6. Four virtual desktops, one screen

If you're working on three projects, for instance, each project can have its own desktop, where you can put all the windows for that project. The pager lets you choose which desktop you want to see. If your window manager has a panel, each virtual desktop probably has its own panel.

Some icons or windows may appear on all desktops; others may appear on just one desktop. For instance, if your system has a console window where you can monitor system log messages, you might want to see that window from every desktop. (Under the Enlightenment window manager, for instance, this is called making a window "stick" to all desktops. On KDE, clicking the push-pin icon near the top left corner of a window frame does the same thing.) But another window—such as a text editor on which you're writing a report about a particular project—should be open only on the desktop where you need it.

By the way, many window-based programs—such as web browsers—can open multiple windows. It's usually more efficient to start the program *just once*, and put its windows on the desktops where you need them, instead of starting a new instance of the program on every desktop. For example, instead of clicking the Netscape icon to start the browser program running on every desktop, click that icon on one desktop and use Netscape's "New Window" command to open multiple windows. You then move each new Netscape window to the desktop where you want it. (In case you need to clear all of the windows from one desktop, though, remember to use Netscape's "Close Window" command instead of its "Quit Netscape" command! Quitting Netscape in this situation would remove all of its windows from *all* of the desktops.)

Unresponsive Windows

While your window system is running, windows may seem to stop responding to commands or mouse clicks. Some or all of the window contents—but not necessarily the window frame itself—may go partly or completely blank. In this case, either a window or the entire window system may be "frozen" or "hung."

The best thing to do in a situation like this is to wait a little while. If the window is showing something from a network, such as a web browser showing a web page from the Internet—or, especially, if the window is from another computer across the network—the cause may be a network delay. If you can wait a minute or two (without pressing extra keys or clicking the mouse around; just wait!) and nothing happens, then it's time to take action. Here are some things to try at that point:

1. Try to find out whether just one window is frozen, or if all windows (and the entire window system) are frozen.

If you have other windows open, try to use them. For instance, if a text editor is open, try to add a word to the text or use a command from one of its menus. If other windows seem to work normally, you can guess that the problem is only in the one window (or family of windows, from one program) that seems frozen.

If you don't have other windows open, try to open a new window from the window manager's menu, icons, panel, etc. Try to minimize and maximize that window, move it around the screen, and so on. If this seems to work normally, the trouble is probably in the original frozen window. But, if nothing seems to work, the whole window system may be frozen.

2. Next, handle the frozen window or windows:

    • If just one window is frozen, you'll probably need to kill it. Click the first mouse button on the "close" box in the window's title bar; this box is often an X symbol. In many Unix window managers, clicking that box sends a "close" signal to the window, and it may do the trick. If it doesn't work, click the third mouse button on that box; in some cases, this will send a "destroy" signal to the window. (All this depends on the window manager you're using!) If several windows are frozen, try these techniques on each window.

      If the windows go away, there's still a chance their Unix processes (the running programs) *haven't* gone away. Or, if the windows *don't* go away, then there probably *are* Unix processes left over. So it's best to check for and kill any leftover processes. In Chapter 7, the section "Cancelling a Process" explains how.

    • If the whole window system is frozen, the computer "underneath" it is probably still running well. Start by trying to close the window system normally from its main menu, with whatever command you normally use. If the whole window system is frozen, that probably won't work.

      The next step is to try to kill your entire X Window System server. You can do this by holding down three keyboard keys at once: CTRL ALT BACKSPACE . If you started the window system from a graphical login, you should see another login box; you can log in again. Or, if you started the window system nongraphically, you should see a shell prompt on your screen; you can repeat the same command (**xinit** or **startx**, for instance) that you used to start the window system before.

If you can't close the window system that way, the last resort is to check for and kill the window system's processes. If you're using a PC operating system such as Linux or NetBSD, try holding down the three keys CTRL ALT F6 ; if you're lucky, you should get a virtual console with a nongraphical "login:" prompt where you can log in and get a shell prompt. Otherwise, you'll probably have to do a remote login from someone else's computer to yours—and get a shell prompt that way. Once you have a shell prompt, read the directions in the section "Cancelling a Process," in Chapter 7; look for processes with names similar to your window manager (such as gnome-session for GNOME).

If you killed windows, or the whole window system—and you were doing work in any of those windows—any changes you made to a file (in a text editor, for instance) may have been lost. It's best to reopen the window, or the whole window system, and check for damage while whatever happened is still fresh in your mind.

Other X Window Programs

Following are a few standard X window programs that your system may have:

- **xbiff**: tells you when new electronic mail comes in
- **xclipboard**: helps with copying and pasting text
- **xmag**: magnifies parts of the screen
- **xman**: browses Unix manual (reference) pages

For more information on those programs and the many other standard X programs, see a reference file or book. There's a list of the X programs that come with XFree86™—and, in general, with other X Releases too—at (as of this printing) *http://www.xfree86.org/current/manindex1.html.*

Quitting

Like almost everything in X, the way to quit X is configurable. The key to shutting down X is to know which of your programs (your windows or window manager) is the *controlling program*. When the controlling program quits, any leftover X programs are killed immediately. The controlling program is usually either the window manager or the single terminal window that started your X session.

Find the controlling program for your X session and write it down:

_____ Program to quit last

If your controlling program is a terminal window, we suggest leaving that window minimized from just after you've logged in until you've shut down all the other X programs. That way, you won't end your X session accidentally by closing that terminal window too soon.

No matter what your controlling program is, closing it sooner than last means the other windows will be killed quickly and automatically. There's a chance, though, that programs running in those killed windows—especially if they're terminal windows—won't be killed, and will keep running, disconnected from your login session. So it's best to close the controlling program window last.

To quit the window manager, select the "Exit" or "Quit" command on its main menu.

Here are the steps to shut down X:

1. Quit all noncontrolling programs (all programs *other* than the controlling program). If any windows are running programs that have their own "quit" commands, it's a good idea to use those special commands to quit. For example, if you're running a text editor in a terminal window, use the editor's "quit" command, then close the terminal window by entering **exit** at the shell prompt. (Most terminal windows will close when their shell program exits. If yours doesn't do this, though, you'll need to finish by using the terminal window's own "close" command.)

    Using the program's own "quit" command gives the program time to clean up and shut down gracefully. On the other hand, the **Close** item on a menu from the window manager can interrupt and kill a program before it's ready. If, however, a program doesn't have its own "quit" command, use **Close** on the window menu.

If any minimized windows are running programs that have their own "quit" commands, restore those windows and use the "quit" command.

2. Quit the controlling program.

    After X shuts down, you may get a Unix shell prompt. If you do, you can log out by entering **exit**. If you simply get another login box from **xdm** (as in Figure 2-2A), you're done.

3

Using Your
Unix Account

Once you log in, you can use the many facilities that Unix provides. As an authorized system user, you have an account that gives you:

- A place in the Unix filesystem where you can store your files.

- A username that identifies you, lets you control access to your files, and is an address for your email.

- An environment you can customize.

The Unix Filesystem

A *file* is the unit of storage in Unix, as in most other systems. A file can hold anything: text (a report you're writing, a to-do list), a program, digitally encoded pictures or sound, and so on. All of those are just sequences of raw data until they're interpreted by the right program.

In Unix, files are organized into directories. A *directory* is actually a special kind of file where the system stores information about other files. You can think of a directory as a place, so that files are said to be contained *in* directories and you are said to work *inside* a directory. (If you've used a Macintosh or Microsoft Windows computer, a Unix directory is similar to a folder.)

This section introduces the Unix filesystem. Later sections in this chapter show how you can look in files and protect them. Chapter 4 has more information.

Your Home Directory

When you log in to Unix, you're placed in a directory called your *home directory*. This directory, a unique place in the Unix filesystem, contains the files you use almost every time you log in. In your home directory, you can make your own files. As you'll see in a minute, you can also store your own directories within your home directory. Like folders in a file cabinet, this is a good way to organize your files.

Your Working Directory

Your *working directory* (also called your current directory) is the directory you're currently working in. Every time you log in, your home directory is your working directory. You may change to another directory, in which case the directory you move to becomes your working directory.

Unless you tell Unix otherwise, all commands that you enter apply to the files in your working directory. In the same way, when you create files, they're created in your working directory unless you specify another directory. For instance, if you type the command pico **report**, the Pico editor is started on a file named *report* in your working directory. But if you type a command such as pico **/home/joan/report**, a *report* file is edited in a different directory—without changing your working directory. You'll learn more about this when we cover pathnames later in this chapter.

If you have more than one terminal window open, or you're logged in on several terminals at the same time, each session has its own working directory. Changing the working directory in one session doesn't affect others.

The Directory Tree

All directories on a Unix system are organized into a hierarchical structure that you can imagine as a family tree. The parent directory of the tree (the directory that contains all other directories) is known as the *root directory* and is written as a forward slash (/).

The root contains several directories. Figure 3-1 shows a visual representation of the top of a Unix filesystem tree: the root directory and some directories under the root.

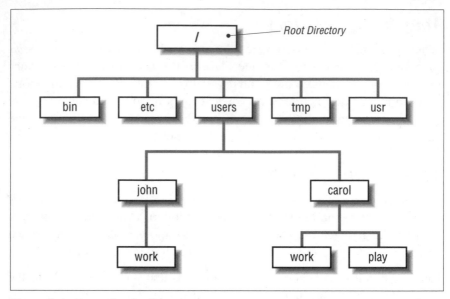

Figure 3-1. Example of a directory tree

bin, etc, users, tmp, and *usr* are some of the subdirectories (child directories) of the root directory. These subdirectories are fairly standard directories; they usually contain specific kinds of system files. For instance, *bin* contains many Unix programs. Not all systems have a directory named *users.* It may be called *u* or *home,* and/or it may be located in some other part of the filesystem.

In our example, the parent directory of *users* (one level above) is the root directory. It has two subdirectories (one level below), *john* and *carol.* On a Unix system, each directory has only one parent directory, but it may have one or more subdirectories.* A subdirectory (such as *carol*) can have its own subdirectories (such as *work* and *play*), up to a limitless depth for practical purposes.

To specify a file or directory location, write its *pathname.* A pathname is like the address of the directory or file in the Unix filesystem. We look at pathnames in a moment.

On a basic Unix system, all files in the filesystem are stored on disks connected to your computer. It isn't always easy to use the files on someone else's computer or for someone on another computer to use your files. Your system may have an easier way: a *networked filesystem.* Networked

---

* On most Unix systems, the root directory, at the top of the tree, is *its own* parent. Some systems have another directory above the root.

filesystems make a remote computer's files appear as if they're part of your computer's directory tree. For instance, a computer in Los Angeles might have a directory named *boston* with some of the directory tree from a company's computer in Boston. Or individual users' home directories may come from various computers, but all be available on your computer as if they were local files. The system staff can help you understand and configure your computer's filesystems to make your work easier.

Absolute Pathnames

As you saw earlier, the Unix filesystem organizes its files and directories in an inverted tree structure with the root directory at the top. An *absolute pathname* tells you the path of directories you must travel to get from the root to the directory or file you want. In a pathname, put slashes (/) between the directory names.

For example, */users/john* is an absolute pathname. It locates one (*only* one!) directory. Here's how:

- The root is the first "/"

- The directory *users* (a subdirectory of *root*)

- The directory *john* (a subdirectory of *users*)

Be sure that you do not type spaces anywhere in the pathname. Figure 3-2 shows this structure.

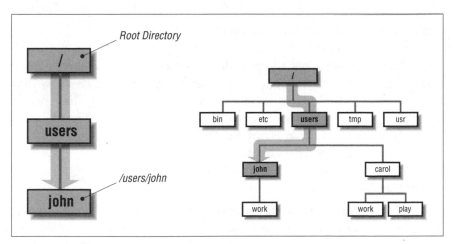

Figure 3-2. Absolute path of directory john

In Figure 3-2, you'll see that the directory *john* has a subdirectory named *work*. Its absolute pathname is */users/john/work*.

The root is always indicated by the slash (/) at the start of the pathname. In other words, *an absolute pathname always starts with a slash.*

Relative Pathnames

You can also locate a file or directory with a *relative pathname*. A relative pathname gives the location relative to your working directory.

Unless you use an absolute pathname (starting with a slash), Unix assumes that you're using a relative pathname. Like absolute pathnames, relative pathnames can go through more than one directory level by naming the directories along the path.

For example, if you're currently in the *users* directory (see Figure 3-2), the relative pathname to the *carol* directory below is simply *carol*. The relative pathname to the *play* directory below that is *carol/play*.

Notice that neither pathname in the previous paragraph starts with a slash. That's what makes them relative pathnames! Relative pathnames start at the working directory, not the root directory. In other words, *a relative pathname never starts with a slash.*

Pathname puzzle

Here's a short but important question. The previous example explains the relative pathname *carol/play*. What do you think Unix would say about the pathname */carol/play*? (Look again at Figure 3-2.)

Unix would say "No such file or directory." Why? (Please think about that before you read more. It's very important and it's one of the most common beginner's mistakes.) Here's the answer. Because it starts with a slash, the pathname */carol/play* is an absolute pathname that starts from the root. It says to look in the root directory for a subdirectory named *carol*. But there is no subdirectory named *carol* one level directly below the root, so the pathname is wrong. The only absolute pathname to the *play* directory is */users/carol/play*.

Relative pathnames up

You can go up the tree with the shorthand ".." (dot dot) for the parent directory. As you saw earlier, you can also go down the tree by using subdirectory names. In either case (up or down), separate each level by a slash (/).

Figure 3-3 shows part of Figure 3-1. If your working directory in the figure is *work*, then there are two pathnames for the *play* subdirectory of *carol*. You already know how to write the absolute pathname, */users/carol/play*. You can also go up one level (with "..") to *carol*, then go down the tree to *play*. Figure 3-3 illustrates this.

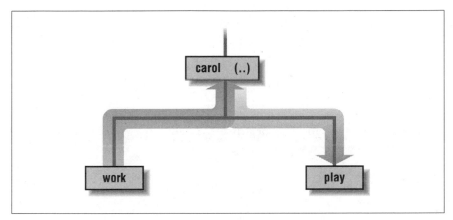

Figure 3-3. Relative pathname from work to play

The relative pathname would be *../play*. It would be wrong to give the relative address as *carol/play*. Using *carol/play* would say that *carol* is a subdirectory of your working directory instead of what it is in this case—the parent directory.

Absolute and relative pathnames are totally interchangeable. Unix programs simply follow whatever path you specify to wherever it leads. If you use an absolute pathname, the path starts from the root. If you use a relative pathname, the path starts from your working directory. Choose whichever is easier at the moment.

Changing Your Working Directory

Once you know the absolute or relative pathname of a directory where you'd like to work, you can move up and down the Unix directory tree to reach it.

pwd

^M To find which directory you're currently in, use **pwd** (print working directory). The **pwd** command takes no arguments.

```
$ pwd
/users/john
$
```

pwd prints the absolute pathname of your working directory.

cd

You can change your working directory to any directory (including another user's directory—if you have permission) with the **cd** (change directory) command.

The **cd** command has the form:

cd *pathname*

The argument is an absolute or a relative pathname (whichever is easier) for the directory you want to change to:

```
$ cd /users/carol
$ pwd
/users/carol
$ cd work
$ pwd
/users/carol/work
$
```

Here's a timesaver: the command **cd**, with no arguments, takes you to your home directory from wherever you are in the filesystem.

Note that you can only change to another directory. You cannot **cd** to a filename. If you try, your shell (in this example, **bash**) gives you an error message:

```
$ cd /etc/passwd
bash: /etc/passwd: Not a directory
$
```

/etc/passwd is a file with information about users' accounts.

Files in the Directory Tree

A directory can hold subdirectories. And, of course, a directory can hold files. Figure 3-4 is a close-up of the filesystem around *john's* home directory. The four files are shown along with the *work* subdirectory.

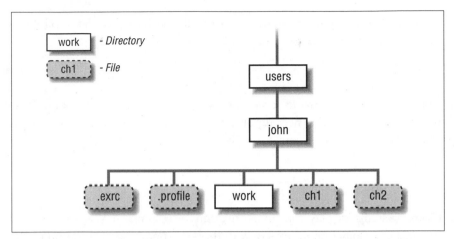

Figure 3-4. Files in the directory tree

Pathnames to files are made the same way as pathnames to directories. As with directories, files' pathnames can be absolute (starting from the root directory) or relative (starting from the working directory). For example, if your working directory is *users*, the relative pathname to the *work* directory below would be *john/work*. The relative pathname to the *ch1* file would be *john/ch1*.

Unix filesystems can hold things that aren't directories or files, such as symbolic links, FIFOs, and sockets (they have pathnames, too). You may see some of them as you explore the filesystem. We don't cover those advanced topics in this little book.

Listing Files with ls

To use the **cd** command, you must decide which entries in a directory are subdirectories and which are files. The **ls** command lists entries in the directory tree and can also show you which is which.

> When you enter the **ls** command, you'll get a listing of the files and subdirectories contained in your working directory. The syntax is:

    ls *option(s) directory-and-filename(s)*

If you've just logged in for the first time, entering **ls** without any arguments may seem to do nothing. This isn't surprising because you haven't made any files in your working directory. If you have no files, nothing is displayed; you'll simply get a new shell prompt:

```
$ ls
$
```

But if you've already made some files or directories in your account, those names are displayed. The output depends on what's in your directory. The screen should look something like this:

```
$ ls
ch1     ch10    ch2     ch3     intro
$
```

(Some systems display filenames in a single column. If yours does, you can make a multicolumn display with the **–C** [uppercase "C"] option or the **–x** option.) ls has a lot of options that change the information and display format.

The **–a** option (for *all*) is guaranteed to show you some more files, as in the following example showing a directory like the one in Figure 3-4:

```
$ ls -a
.         .exrc    ch1     ch2     intro
..        .profile ch10    ch3
$
```

When you use ls -a, you'll always see at least two entries with the names "." (dot) and ".." (dot dot). As mentioned earlier, .. is always the relative pathname to the parent directory. A single . always stands for its working directory; this is useful with commands like **cp** (see the section "Copying Files" in Chapter 4). There may also be other files, such as *.profile* or *.exrc*. Any entry whose name begins with a dot is hidden—it's listed only if you use ls -a.

To get more information about each item that ls lists, add the **–l** option. (That's a lowercase "L" for "long.") This option can be used alone, or in combination with **–a**, as shown in Figure 3-5.

The long format provides the following information about each item:

Total n

> *n* amount of storage used by everything in this directory. (This is measured in *blocks*. On many systems, but not all, a full block holds 1024 bytes. A block can also be partly full.)

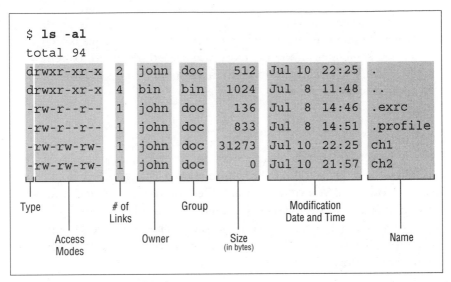

```
$ ls -al
total 94
drwxr-xr-x  2  john  doc    512  Jul 10  22:25  .
drwxr-xr-x  4  bin   bin   1024  Jul  8  11:48  ..
-rw-r--r--  1  john  doc    136  Jul  8  14:46  .exrc
-rw-r--r--  1  john  doc    833  Jul  8  14:51  .profile
-rw-rw-rw-  1  john  doc  31273  Jul 10  22:25  ch1
-rw-rw-rw-  1  john  doc      0  Jul 10  21:57  ch2
```

Type

Access
Modes

\# of
Links

Owner

Group

Size
(in bytes)

Modification
Date and Time

Name

Figure 3-5. Output from ls -al

Type

Tells whether the item is a directory (d) or a plain file (–). (There are
other less common types that we don't explain here.)

Access modes

Specifies three types of users (yourself, your group, all others) who
are allowed to read (r), write (w), or execute (x) your files. We'll say
more about this in a moment.

Links

The number of files or directories linked to this one. (This isn't the
same sort of *link* as in a web page. We don't discuss filesystem links
in this little book.)

Owner

The user who created or owns this file or directory.

Group

The group that owns the file or directory. (If your version of Unix
doesn't show this column, add the **-g** option to see it.)

Size (in bytes)

The size of the file or directory. (A directory is actually a special type
of file. Here, the "size" of a directory is of the directory file itself, not
of all the files in that directory.)

Modification date

When the file was last modified, or the directory contents last changed (when something in the directory was added, renamed, or removed). If an entry was modified more than six months ago, ls shows the year instead of the time.

Name

The name of the file or directory.

Notice especially the columns that list the owner and group of the files, and the access modes (also called permissions). The person who creates a file is its owner; if you've created any files (or system staff did it for you), this column should show your username. You also belong to a group, set by the person who created your account. Files you create are either marked with the name of your group, or in some cases, the group that owns the directory.

The *permissions* show who can read, write, or execute the file or directory; we explain what that means in a moment. The permissions have ten characters. The first character shows the file type (d for directory or – for a plain file). The other characters come in groups of three. The first group, characters 2–4, show the permissions for the file's owner, which is yourself if you created the file. The second group, characters 5–7, show permissions for other members of the file's group. The third group, characters 8–10, show permissions for all other users.

For example, the permissions for *.profile* are –rw-r--r--, so it's a plain file. The owner, *john*, has both read and write permissions. Other users who belong to the file's group *doc*, as well as all other users of the system, can only read the file; they don't have write permission, so they can't change what's in the file. No one has execute (x) permission, which should only be used for executable files (files that hold programs).

In the case of directories, x means the permission to access the directory—for example, to run a command that reads a file there or to use a subdirectory. Notice that the two directories shown in the example are executable (accessible) by *john*, by users in the *doc* group, and by everyone else on the system. A directory with w (write) permission allows deleting, renaming, or adding files within the directory. Read (r) permission allows listing the directory with ls.

You can use the **chmod** command to change the permissions of your files and directories. See the section "Protecting and Sharing Files," later in this chapter.

If you need to know only which files are directories and which are executable files, you can use the **-F** option.

If you give the pathname to a directory, **ls** lists the directory but it does *not* change your working directory. The **pwd** command in the following example shows this:

```
$ ls -F /users/andy
calendar    goals    ideas/
ch2         guide/   testpgm*
$ pwd
/etc
$
```

ls -F puts a / (slash) at the end of each directory name. (The directory name doesn't really have a slash in it; that's just the shortcut **ls** -F uses to identify a directory.) In our example, *guide* and *ideas* are directories. You can verify this by using **ls** -l and noting the "d" in the first field of the output. Files with an execute status (x), such as programs, are marked with an * (asterisk). The file *testpgm* is an executable file. Files that aren't marked are not executable.

ls -R ("recursive") lists a directory and all its subdirectories. This can make a very long list—especially when you list a directory near the root! (Piping the output of **ls** to a pager program solves this problem. There's an example in the section "Piping to a Pager" in Chapter 5.) You can combine other options with **-R**: for instance, **ls** -RF marks each directory and file type.

On Linux and other systems with the GNU version of **ls**, you may be able to see names in color. For instance, directories could be green and program files could be yellow. Like almost everything on Unix, of course, this is configurable. The details are more than we can cover in an introductory book. Try typing **ls** --color and see what happens. (It's time for our familiar mantra: check your documentation. See Chapter 8—especially the **man** command for reading a command's online manual page.)

Exercise: exploring the filesystem

You're now equipped to explore the filesystem with **cd**, **ls**, and **pwd**. Take a tour of the directory system, hopping one or many levels at a time, with a mixture of **cd** and **pwd** commands.

Go to your home directory.	Enter **cd**
Find your working directory.	Enter **pwd**
Change to new working directory with its absolute pathname.	Enter **cd /etc**
List files in new working directory.	Enter **ls**
Change directory to root and list it in one step. (Use the command separator, a semicolon.)	Enter **cd /; ls**
Find your working directory.	Enter **pwd**
Change to a subdirectory; use its relative pathname.	Enter **cd usr**
Find your working directory.	Enter **pwd**
Change to a subdirectory.	Enter **cd bin**
Find your working directory.	Enter **pwd**
Give a wrong pathname.	Enter **cd xqk**
List files in another directory.	Enter **ls /bin**
Find your working directory (notice that **ls** didn't change it).	Enter **pwd**
Return to your home directory.	Enter **cd**

Looking Inside Files with less

By now, you're probably tired of looking at files from the outside. It's kind of like going to a bookstore and looking at the covers, but never getting to read a word. Let's look at a program for reading files.

If you want to "read" a long file on the screen, your system may have the **less** command to display one "page" (a terminal filled from top to bottom) of text at a time.

If you don't have **less**, you'll probably have similar programs named **more** or **pg**. (In fact, the name **less** is a play on the name of **more**, which came first.) The syntax is:

> **less** *option(s) file(s)*

less lets you move forward or backward in the files by any number of pages or lines; you can also move back and forth between two or more files specified on the command line. When you invoke **less**, the first "page" of the file appears. A prompt appears at the bottom of the terminal (or terminal window), as in the following example:

```
$ less ch03
A file is the unit of storage in Unix, as in most other systems.
A file can hold anything: text (a report you're writing,
        .
        .
        .
    :
```

The basic **less** prompt is just a colon (:)—although, for the first screenful, **less** displays the file's name as a prompt. The cursor sits to the right of this prompt as a signal for you to enter a **less** command to tell **less** what to do.

Like almost everything about **less**, the prompt can be customized. For example, using the **less -M** option on the **less** command line makes the prompt show the filename and your position in the file. (If you want this to happen every time you use **less**, you can set the LESS environment variable to M (without a dash) in your shell setup file. See the section "Customizing Your Account," later in this chapter.)

You can set or unset most options temporarily from the **less** prompt. For instance, if you have the short **less** prompt (a colon), you can enter **-M** while **less** is running. **less** responds "Long prompt (press RETURN)," and for the rest of the session, **less** prompts with the filename, line number, and percentage of the file viewed.

To display the **less** commands and options available on your system, press "h" (for "help") while **less** is running. Table 3-1 lists some simple (but still quite useful) commands.

Table 3-1. Useful less commands

Command	Description	Command	Description
SPACE	Display next page.	v	v
RETURN	Display next line.	CTRL-L	Redisplay current page.
*n*f	Move forward *n* lines.		Help.
	Move backward one page.	:n	Go to next file on command line.
*n*b	Move backward *n* lines.	:p	Go back to previous file on command line.
/*word*	Search forward for *word*.	q	Quit **less**.
?*word*	Search backward for *word*.		

Protecting and Sharing Files

Unix makes it easy for users to share files and directories. For instance, everyone in a group can read documents stored in one of their manager's directories without needing to make their own copies—if the manager has allowed access. There might be no need to fill peoples' email inboxes with file attachments if everyone can access those files directly through the Unix filesystem.

Here's a brief introduction to file security and sharing. Networked systems with multiple users, such as Unix, have complex security issues that take tens or hundreds of pages to explain. If you have critical security needs or you just want more information, talk to your system staff or see an up-to-date book on Unix security.

Note that the system's superuser (the system administrator and possibly other users) can do anything to any file at any time, no matter what its permissions are. So, access permissions won't keep your private information safe from *everyone*—although let's hope that you can trust your system staff!

Your system staff should also keep backup copies of users' files. These backup copies may be readable by anyone who has physical access to them. That is, anyone who can take the backup out of a cabinet (or wherever) and mount it on a computer system may be able to read the file copies. The same is true for files stored on floppy disks and any other removable media. (Once you take a file off of a Unix system, that system can't control access to it anymore.)

Directory Access Permissions

A directory's access permissions help to control access to the files and subdirectories in that directory:

- If a directory has read permission, a user can run **ls** to see what's in the directory and use wildcards to match files in it.

- A directory that has write permission allows users to add, rename, and delete files in the directory.

- To access a directory—that is, to read or write the files in the directory or to run the files if they're programs—a user needs execute permission on that directory. Note that to access a directory, a user must *also* have execute permission to all of its parent directories, all the way up to the root!

File Access Permissions

The access permissions on a file control what can be done to the file's *contents*. The access permissions on the *directory* where the file is kept control whether the file can be renamed or removed. (If this seems confusing, think of it this way: the directory is actually a list of files. Adding, renaming, or removing a file changes the contents of the directory. If the directory isn't writable, you can't change that list.)

Read permission controls whether you can read a file's contents. Write permission lets you change a file's contents. A file shouldn't have execute permission unless it's a program.

Setting Permissions with chmod

Once you know what permissions a file or directory needs—and if you're the owner (listed in the third column of **ls –l** output)—you can change the permissions with the **chmod** program.

There are two ways to change permissions: by specifying the permissions to add or delete, or by specifying the exact permissions.* For instance, if a directory's permissions are almost correct, but you also need to make it writable by its group, tell **chmod** to add group-write permission. But if you need to make more than one change to the permissions—for instance, you want to add read and execute permission, but delete write permission—it's easier to set all permissions explicitly instead of changing them one-by-one. The syntax is:

 chmod *permissions file(s)*

Let's start with the rules; we see examples next. The *permissions* argument has three parts, which you must give in order with no space between.

---

* Early versions of **chmod** can't add or delete particular permissions. Instead, you have to give an exact permission as three digits between 0 and 7. If you need to use **chmod** that way, please see a more detailed Unix reference.

1. The category of permission you want to change. There are three: the owner's permission (which **chmod** calls "user," abbreviated u), the group's permission (g), or others' permission (o). To change more than one category, string the letters together, such as go for "group and others," or simply use a to mean "all" (same as ugo).

2. Whether you want to add (+) the permission, delete (–) it, or specify it exactly (=).

3. What permissions you want to affect: read (r), write (w), or execute (x). To change more than one permission, string the letters together—for example, rw for "read and write."

Some examples should make this clearer! In the following command lines, you can replace *dirname* or *filename* with the pathname (absolute or relative) of the directory or file. An easy way to change permissions on the working directory is by using its relative pathname, . (dot), as in "**chmod a-w .**". You can combine two permission changes in the same **chmod** command by separating them with a comma (,), as shown in the final example.

*   To protect a file from accidental editing, delete everyone's write permission with the command "**chmod a-w** *filename*". On the other hand, if you own an unwritable file that you want to edit, but you don't want to change other peoples' write permissions, you can add "user" (owner) write permission with "**chmod u+w** *filename*".

*   To keep yourself from accidentally removing files (or adding or renaming files) in an important directory of yours, delete your own write permission with the command "**chmod u-w** *dirname*". If other users have that permission, too, you could delete everyone's write permission with "**chmod a-w** *dirname*".

*   If you want you and your group to be able to read and write all the files in your working directory—but those files have various permissions now, so adding and deleting the permissions individually would be a pain—this is a good place to use the = operator to set the exact permissions you want. Use the filename wildcard *, which means "everything in this directory" (explained in the section "File and Directory Wildcards" of Chapter 4) and type: "**chmod ug=rw** *"*.

If your working directory had any subdirectories, though, that command would be wrong because it takes away execute permission from the subdirectories, so the subdirectories couldn't be accessed anymore. In that case, you could try a more specific wildcard. Or, instead of a wildcard, you can simply list the filenames you want to change, separated by spaces, as in "**chmod ug=rw afile bfile cfile**".

- To protect the files in a directory and all its subdirectories from everyone else on your system, but still keep the access permissions *you* have there, you could use "**chmod go-rwx** *dirname*" in order to delete all "group" and "others" permission to read, write, and execute. A simpler way is to use the command "**chmod go=** *dirname*" to set "group" and "others" permission to exactly nothing.

- You want full access to a directory. Other people on the system should be able to see what's in the directory—and read or edit the files if the file permissions allow it—but not rename, remove, or add files. To do that, give yourself all permissions, but give "group" and "others" only read and execute permission. Use the command "**chmod u=rwx,go=rx** *dirname*".

After you change permissions, it's a good idea to check your work at first with "**ls -l** *filename*" or "**ls -ld** *dirname*".

More Protection Under Linux

Most Linux systems have a program named **chattr** that gives you more choices on file and directory protection. **chattr** is being developed, and your version may not have all the features that it will have in later Linux versions. For instance, **chattr** can make a Linux file *append-only* (so it can't be overwritten, only added to), *compressed* (to save disk space automatically), *immutable* (so it can't be changed at all), *undeletable*, and more. Check your online documentation (type **man chattr**—see Chapter 8).

Problem checklist

I get the message "chmod: Not owner."

Only the owner of a file or directory—or the superuser—can set its permissions. Use **ls -l** to find the owner, or ask a system staff person to change the permissions.

A file is writable, but my program says it can't be written.

First, check the file permissions with **ls -l** and be sure you're in the category (user, group, or others) that has write permission.

The problem may also be in the permissions of the file's *directory*. Some programs need permission to write more files into the same directory (for example, temporary files), or to rename files (for instance, making a file into a backup) while editing. If it's safe to add write permission to the directory (if other files in the directory don't need protection from removal or renaming) try that. Otherwise, copy the file to a writable directory (with **cp**), edit it there, then copy it back to the original directory.

Changing Group and Owner

Group ownership lets a certain group of users have access to a file or directory. You might need to let a different group have access. The **chgrp** program sets the group owner of a file or directory. You can set the group to any of the groups you belong to. (The system staff control the list of groups you're in.) On most versions of Unix, the **groups** program lists your groups.

For example, if you're an instructor creating a directory named *csc303* for students in a course, the directory's original group owner might be *faculty*. You'd like the students, all of whom are in the group named *csstudnt*, to access the directory; members of other groups should have no access. Use commands such as these:*

```
$ groups
faculty csstudnt wheel research
$ mkdir csc303
$ ls -ld csc303
drwxr-xr-x    2 roberts    faculty      4096 Aug 25 13:35 csc303
$ chgrp csstudnt csc303
$ chmod o= csc303
$ ls -ld csc303
drwxr-x---    2 roberts    csstudnt     4096 Aug 25 13:35 csc303
```

The **chown** program changes the owner of a file or directory. On most Unix systems, only the superuser can use **chown**.†

---

* Many Unix systems also let you set a directory's group ownership so that any files you later create in that directory will be owned by the same group as the directory. Try the command "chmod **g+s** *dirname*". If this works, the permissions listing from ls –ld should show an *s* in place of the second *x*, such as drwxr-s---.

† If you have permission to read another user's file, you can make a copy of it (with **cp**; see the section "Copying Files" in Chapter 4). You'll own the copy.

Graphical Filesystem Browsers

Most Unix window systems give you a graphical way to do some of the things you can do with files from the command line. A *filesystem browser*, such as the GNOME File Manager or KDE's Konqueror, lets you see a graphical representation of the filesystem and do a limited number of operations on it. Figure 3-6 shows the GNOME filesystem browser. The left pane has a directory tree. The right pane shows the contents of the directory that's selected (open) in the left pane; here, this is the directory */home/mpeek*. The titlebar shows the pathname of the selected directory.

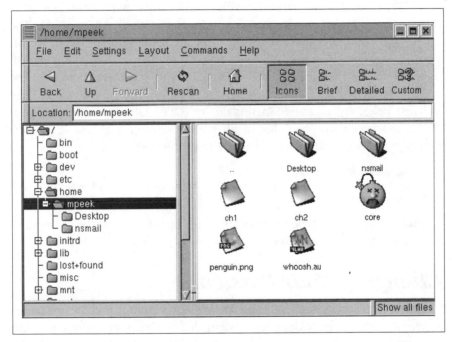

Figure 3-6. GNOME filesystem browser

A filesystem browser can be handy for seeing what's in the filesystem. Unfortunately, because a filesystem browser takes you away from the shell you're using for other work, it can limit what you're able to do with Unix. (You'll see additional information about why this is true when we cover more advanced features such as input-output redirection in Chapter 5.) We recommend learning about your filesystem browser but also learning what you can do at the more powerful Unix command line.

Completing File and Directory Names

Most Unix shells can complete a partly typed file or directory name for you. Different shells have different methods. In many shells, you type the first few letters of the name, then press $\boxed{\text{TAB}}$. If the shell can find just one way to finish the name, it will; your cursor will move to the end of the new name, where you can type more or press $\boxed{\text{RETURN}}$ to run the command. (You also can edit or erase the completed name.)

What happens if more than one file or directory name matches what you've typed so far? Again, that depends on the shell you're using. The cursor will probably stay where it is, and the terminal may beep. At this point, the easiest answer could be to type more characters of the name (to make the name unique) and press $\boxed{\text{TAB}}$ again to complete the rest of the name. You may also be able to get a list of all possible completions; after the first beep, try pressing $\boxed{\text{TAB}}$ again (or $\boxed{\text{CTRL-D}}$, depending on your shell) and you may see a list of all names starting with the characters you've typed so far. Here's an example from the **bash** shell:

```
$ cp /etc/pa TAB (beep) TAB
pam.d           paper.config  passwd        passwd-       passwd.OLD
$ cp /etc/pa
```

At this point, I could type another character or two—an *s*, for example—and then press $\boxed{\text{TAB}}$ once more to make /etc/passwd.

Changing Your Password

On most Unix systems, everyone knows (or can find) your username. When you log in, how does the system decide that you really own your account and aren't an intruder trying to break in? Unix uses your password. If anyone knows both your username and password, they can use your account—including sending email that looks as if you wrote it.* So you should keep your password a secret! Never write it down and leave it anywhere near your terminal.

If you think that someone knows your password, you should probably change it right away—although, if you suspect a computer "cracker" (or

---

* Unfortunately, it's easy to forge email, without using your computer account at all, so that no one but an expert can tell it was forged.

"hacker") is using your account to break into your system, ask your system administrator for advice first, if possible! You should also change your password periodically; every few months is recommended.

A password should be easy for you to remember but hard for other people (or password-guessing programs!) to guess. Your system should have guidelines for secure passwords. If it doesn't, here are some suggestions. A password should be between six and eight characters long. It should *not* be a word in *any* language, your phone number, your address, or anything anyone else might know or guess that you'd use as a password. It's best to mix upper- and lowercase letters, punctuation, and numbers.

To change your password, you'll probably use either the *passwd* or *yppasswd* program from a shell prompt. After you enter the command, it prompts you to enter your password ("old password"). If the password is correct, it asks you to enter your new password—twice, to be sure there is no typing mistake. For security, neither the old nor new passwords appear as you type them.

On some systems, your password change won't take effect for some time. The change may require between a few minutes to a day.

Customizing Your Account

As we saw earlier, your home directory may have a hidden file called *.profile*. If it doesn't, there'll probably be one or more files named *.login*, *.cshrc*, *.tcshrc*, *.bashrc*, *.bash_profile*, or *.bash_login*. These files are *shell setup files*, and are the key to customizing your account. Shell setup files contain commands that are automatically executed when a new shell starts—especially when you log in.

Let's take a look at these files. Go to your home directory, then use **less** to display the file. Your *.profile* might look something like this:

```
PATH='/bin:/usr/bin:/usr/local/bin:'
LESS='eMq'
export PATH LESS
/usr/games/fortune
date
umask 002
```

A *.login* file could look like this:

```
set path = (/bin /usr/bin /usr/local/bin .)
setenv LESS 'eMq'
/usr/games/fortune
date
umask 002
```

As you can see, these sample setup files contain commands to print a "fortune" and the date—just what happened earlier when we logged in! (*/usr/ games/fortune* is a useless but entertaining program that prints a randomly selected saying from its collection. **fortune** isn't available on all systems.)

But what are these other commands?

- The line with PATH= or set path = tells the shell which directories to search for Unix programs. This saves you the trouble of typing the complete pathname for each program you run. (Notice that */usr/ games* isn't part of the path, so we had to use the absolute pathname to get our daily dose of wisdom from the **fortune** program.) The export PATH is needed in the *.profile*, but not in *.login.**

- The line with LESS= or setenv LESS tells the **less** program which options you want to set every time you use it. This saves you the trouble of typing the options on every **less** command line. The export LESS line is needed in the *.profile*, but not in *.login.*

- The **umask** command sets the default file permissions assigned to all files you create. Briefly, a value of 022 sets the permissions rw-r--r-- (read-write by owner, but read-only by everyone else), and 002 produces rw-rw-r-- (read-write by owner and group, but read-only by everyone else). If this file is a program or a directory, both **umask** settings also give execute (x) permission to all users. For more information, see one of the sources in the section "Documentation" of Chapter 8.

You can change these files with a text editor, such as **pico -w** (see the section "The Pico Text Editor" in Chapter 4). Don't use a word processor that breaks long lines or puts special nontext codes into the file. Any changes you make to those files will take effect the next time you log in (or, in some cases, when you start a new shell—such as opening a new terminal window in your window system). Unfortunately, it's not always easy to know which shell setup file you should change.† And an editing mistake in your shell setup file can keep you from logging in to your account! We suggest that beginners get help from experienced users—and not make changes to these files at all if you're about to do some critical work with your account, unless there's some reason you have to make the changes immediately.

---

* Some shells that read the *.profile* let you set a variable's value on the same line as the **export** command, but not all do. Our two-step method for setting PATH works in all cases.

† Some files are read by *login shells*, and others by *nonlogin shells*. Some are read by *subshells*; others aren't. Some terminal windows open login shells; others don't.

You can execute any of these programs from the command line, as well. In this case, the changes are in effect only until you close that window or log out. If your shell prompt has a $ character in it, you'll probably use the syntax shown earlier in the *.profile*; if your shell prompt has a % or > instead, the syntax in the *.login* is probably right.

For example, to change the default options for **less** so it will clear the terminal screen before it shows each new page of text, you'll want to add the -c option to the LESS environment variable. The command you'd type at a shell prompt would look something like this:

```
$ LESS='eMqc'
$ export LESS
```

or like this:

```
% setenv LESS 'eMqc'
```

(If you don't want some of the **less** options we've shown, you could leave those letters out.) Unix has many other configuration commands to learn about; the sources listed in the section "Documentation" of Chapter 8 can help.

Just as you can execute the setup commands from the command line, the converse is true: any command that you can execute from the command line can be executed automatically when you log in by placing it in your setup file. (Running interactive commands such as **pine** from your setup file isn't a good idea, though.)

4

File Management

Chapter 3 introduced the Unix filesystem. This chapter explains how to name, edit, copy, move, find, and print files.

File and Directory Names

As Chapter 3 explains, both files and directories are identified by their names. A directory is really just a special kind of file, so the rules for naming directories are the same as the rules for naming files.

Filenames may contain any character except /, which is reserved as the separator between files and directories in a pathname. Filenames are usually made of upper- and lowercase letters, numbers, "." (dots), and "_" (underscores). Other characters (including spaces) are legal in a filename, but they can be hard to use because the shell gives them special meanings. So we recommend using only letters, numbers, dots, and underscore characters. You can also use "–" (dashes), as long as they aren't the first character of a filename, which can make a program think the filename is an option.

If you have a file with a space in its name, the shell will be confused if you type its name on the command line. That's because the shell breaks command lines into separate arguments at the spaces.

To tell the shell not to break an argument at spaces, put quote marks (") around the argument. For example, the **rm** program, covered later in this chapter, removes files.

To remove a file named *a confusing name*, the first **rm** command, which follows, doesn't work; the second one does:

```
$ ls -l
total 2
-rw-r--r--  1  jpeek users     0 Oct 23 11:23 a confusing name
-rw-r--r--  1  jpeek users  1674  Oct 23 11:23 ch01
$ rm a confusing name
rm: a: no such file or directory
rm: confusing: no such file or directory
rm: name: no such file or directory
$ rm "a confusing name"
$
```

Unlike some operating systems, Unix doesn't require a dot (.) in a filename; in fact, you can use as many as you want. For instance, the filenames *pizza* and *this.is.a.mess* are both legal.

Some Unix systems limit filenames to 14 characters. Most newer systems allow much longer filenames.

A filename must be unique inside its directory, but other directories may have files with the same names. For example, you may have the files called *chap1* and *chap2* in the directory */users/carol/work* and also have files with the same names in */users/carol/play*.

File and Directory Wildcards

When you have a number of files named in series (for example, *chap1* to *chap12*) or filenames with common characters (such as *aegis, aeon,* and *aerie*), you can use *wildcards* to specify many files at once. These special characters are * (asterisk), ? (question mark), and [ ] (square brackets). When used in a file or directory name given as an argument on a command line, the following is true:

*   An asterisk stands for any number of characters in a filename. For example, *ae** would match *aegis, aerie, aeon,* etc. if those files were in the same directory. You can use this to save typing for a single filename (for example, *al** for *alphabet.txt*) or to choose many files at once (as in *ae**). A * by itself matches all file and subdirectory names in a directory.

?   A question mark stands for any single character (so *h?p* matches *hop* and *hip*, but not *help*).

[ ] Square brackets can surround a choice of single characters (i.e., one digit or one letter) you'd like to match. For example, *[Cc]hapter* would match either *Chapter* or *chapter*, but *[ch]apter* would match either *capter* or *hapter*. Use a hyphen (–) to separate a range of consecutive characters. For example, *chap[1–3]* would match *chap1*, *chap2*, or *chap3*.

The following examples show the use of wildcards. The first command lists all the entries in a directory, and the rest use wildcards to list just some of the entries. The last one is a little tricky; it matches files whose names contain two (or more) *a*'s.

```
$ ls
chap10        chap2        chap5      cold
chap1a.old    chap3.old    chap6      haha
chap1b        chap4        chap7      oldjunk
$ ls chap?
chap2     chap5     chap7
chap4     chap6
$ ls chap[5-7]
chap5     chap6     chap7
$ ls chap[5-9]
chap5     chap6     chap7
$ ls chap??
chap10    chap1b
$ ls *old
chap1a.old    chap3.old    cold
$ ls *a*a*
chap1a.old    haha
```

Wildcards are useful for more than listing files. Most Unix programs accept more than one filename, and you can use wildcards to name multiple files on the command line. For example, the **less** program displays a file on the screen. Let's say you want to display files *chap3.old* and *chap1a.old*. Instead of specifying these files individually, you could enter the command as:

```
$ less *.old
```

This is equivalent to "**less chap1a.old chap3.old**".

Wildcards match directory names, too. You can use them anywhere in a pathname—absolute or relative—though you still need to separate directory levels with slashes (/). For example, let's say you have subdirectories named *Jan*, *Feb*, *Mar*, and so on. Each has a file named *summary*. You could read all the summary files by typing "**less */summary**". That's almost equivalent to "**less Jan/summary Feb/summary** . . . " but there's one important difference: the names will be alphabetized, so *Apr/summary* would be first in the list.

Creating and Editing Files

One easy way to create a file is with a Unix feature called *input/output redirection*, as Chapter 5 explains. This sends the output of a program directly to a file, to make a new file or add to an existing one.

You'll usually create and edit a plain-text file with a *text editor* program. Text editors are somewhat different than *word processors*.

Text Editors and Word Processors

A *text editor* lets you add, change, and rearrange text easily. Two common Unix editors are **vi** (pronounced "vee-eye") and **emacs** ("ee-macs"). **Pico** ("pea-co") is a simple editor that has been added to many Unix systems.

Since there are several editor programs, you can choose one you're comfortable with. **vi** is probably the best choice because almost all Unix systems have it, but **emacs** is also widely available. If you'll be doing simple editing only, **pico** is a great choice. Although **pico** is much less powerful than **emacs** or **vi**, it's also a lot easier to learn.

None of those editors has the same features as popular word processing software on personal computers. **vi** and **emacs** are sophisticated, extremely flexible editors for all kinds of plain text files: programs, email messages, and so on.

By "plain text," we mean a file with only letters, numbers, and punctuation characters in it. Unix systems use plain text files in many places: redirected input and output of Unix programs (Chapter 5), as shell setup files (see the section "Customizing Your Account" in Chapter 3), for shell scripts (shown in the section "Programming" of Chapter 8), for system configuration, and more. Text editors edit these files. When you use a word processor, though, although the screen may look as if the file is only plain text, the file probably also has hidden codes (nontext characters) in it. That's often true even if you tell the word processor to "Save as plain text." One easy way to check for nontext characters in a file is by reading the file with **less**; look for characters in reversed colors, codes like <36>, and so on.

If you need to do word processing—making documents, envelopes, and so on—most Unix systems also support easy-to-use word processors such

as WordPerfect and StarOffice (which are compatible, more or less, with
Microsoft word processors). Ask your system staff what's available or can
be installed.

The Pico Text Editor

The Pico editor, from the University of Washington, is easy to use. If you
send email with Pine, you already know how to use Pico; it's Pine's message editor. Like Pine, Pico is still evolving; if you use an older version
than we did here (Version 3.7), yours may have some different features.

Start Pico by typing its name; the argument is the filename you want to
create or edit. If you're editing a Unix shell setup file or shell script, you'll
also want the **-w** option; it tells Pico not to break ("wrap") lines at the
right margin, but only when you press the RETURN key. If a line is
longer than the right margin, like the line starting with PATH= in Figure 4-1,
pico -w marks the right end with a dollar sign ($). When you move the
cursor over the dollar sign, the next 80 characters of that one line are displayed. For instance, to edit my *.profile* setup file, I **cd** to my home directory and enter:

```
$ pico -w .profile
```

My terminal fills with a copy of the file (and, because the file is short,
some blank lines too), as shown in Figure 4-1.

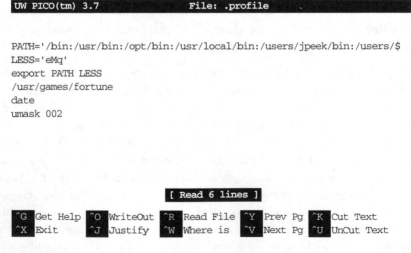

Figure 4-1. Pico display while editing

The bottom two rows of the window list some Pico commands. For example, CTRL-J justifies the paragraph you're editing, making the lines fit neatly between the margins. For a complete list of commands, use CTRL-G , the "Get Help" command.

Pico tour

Let's take a tour through Pico. In this example, you'll make a new file with wrapped lines. So (unlike what you'd do when editing a system setup file) we *won't* use the -w option. You can call the file anything you want, but it's best to use only letters and numbers in the filename. For instance, to make a file named *sample*, enter the command **pico sample**. Let's start our tour now.

1. Your screen should look something like the previous example, but the middle of the screen should be blank, ready for you to enter text.

2. Enter some lines of text. Make some lines too short (press RETURN before the line gets to the right margin). Make others too long; watch how Pico wraps long lines. If you're using a window system and you have another terminal window open with some text in it, you can also use your mouse to copy text from another window and paste it into the Pico window. (Chapter 2 includes the section "Using a Mouse with xterm Windows," which has instructions for copying and pasting between **xterm** windows.) To get a lot of text quickly, paste the same text more than once.

3. Let's practice moving around the file. Pico works on all terminals, with or without a mouse, so it will probably ignore your mouse if you try to use it to move the cursor. Instead, use the keyboard to move the cursor. If your keyboard has arrow keys, they'll probably move the cursor. Otherwise, try the cursor-moving commands listed in the help page, such as CTRL-F to move forward a character, CTRL-E to move to the end of a line, and CTRL-A to go to the start of a line. If your PAGE UP and PAGE DOWN keys don't work, use CTRL-Y and CTRL-V , respectively.

    Pico's search or "where is" command, CTRL-W , can help you find a word quickly. It's handy even on a short file, where it can be quicker to type CTRL-W and a word than to use the cursor-moving commands. The search command is also a good example of the way that **pico** can change its display momentarily. Let's try it. Type CTRL-W ; you should see a display like Figure 4-2.

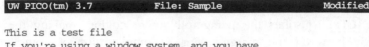

```
This is a test file
If you're using a window system, and you have
another terminal window open with some text in it, you can also
use your mouse to copy text from another window and paste it
into the Pico window.

If you're using a window system, and
you have another terminal window open with some text in it,
you can also use your mouse to copy text from another window
and paste it into the Pico window.
```

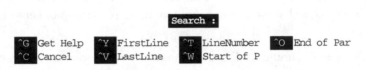

Figure 4-2. Pico display while searching

Notice that the command list at the bottom of the display has changed since you started Pico (Figure 4-1). The cursor sits after the word "Search:". You can type a word or characters to search for, then press RETURN to do the search. You also can do any other command listed, such as CTRL-T to go to a particular line number. Type CTRL-G to get a help display. Notice that if you type CTRL-W while the search command is active, it doesn't start another search; it goes to the start of the current paragraph. After a search finishes, you can type CTRL-W again, then press RETURN to repeat the search.

4. If your text isn't in paragraphs separated by blank lines, break some of it into paragraphs. Put your cursor at the place you want to break the text and press RETURN twice (once to break the line, another to make a blank line).

    Now justify one paragraph. Put the cursor somewhere in it and press CTRL-J. Now the paragraph's lines should flow and fit neatly between the margins.

5. Because **pico** doesn't use a mouse, cutting/copying and pasting text works differently than it does with mouse-based editors you might have used before. Please choose some text to copy or cut, then paste.

    The first step is to select the text to cut or copy. Move the cursor to the first character, then press CTRL-^ (control followed by the caret key, ^).

Move the cursor to the last character you want and press CTRL-K .
That cuts the text. Pico will "remember" the text you cut and let you
paste it back as many times as you want until you cut some other text
(or until you quit your **pico** session).

If you only wanted to copy the text, not to cut it, you can paste the
text back where you cut it. Press CTRL-U to "uncut"—that is,
paste—the text at current cursor position.

Or, if you wanted to move the text somewhere else, move the cursor
to that spot and press CTRL-U there.

6. As with any text editor, it's a good idea to save your work from **pico**
    every few minutes. That way, if something goes wrong on the com-
    puter or network, you'll only lose the work since the last time you
    saved it. (Pico saves interrupted work in a file named *pico.save* or
    filename.save, where *filename* is the name of the file you were edit-
    ing. But I like to save by hand when I know that the file is in a good
    state.)

Try writing out your work with CTRL-O . The bottom of the display
will look like Figure 4-3. The cursor sits after the name of the file
you're editing.

This part confuses some pico beginners. If you want to save the file
with the same name it had as you started, just press RETURN ; that's
all! You can also choose a *different* filename.

One way to use a different filename is to edit the filename in place.
For instance, if you want to call the backup copy *sample1*, simply
press the *1* key to add a *1* to the end of the filename before you press
RETURN to save it.

You can backspace over the name and type a new one. Or move to
the start or middle of the name by using the arrow keys, CTRL-B and
CTRL-F , then add or delete characters in the name. As an example,
you could edit the filename to be an absolute pathname such as
/home/carol/backups/sample.

If you choose CTRL-T , "To Files," you'll go to a file browser where
you can look through a list of your files and directories. You also can
type part of an existing filename and use filename completion (see
the section "Completing File and Directory Names" in Chapter 3). By
default, filename completion assumes that you started Pico from your
home directory—even if you didn't. (You can change this with the
use-current-dir preference setting for Pine—which also affects Pico.
See the section "Configuring Pine" in Chapter 6.)

7. Make one or two more small edits. Then exit with CTRL-X . Pico prompts you to save the file; see the explanation of CTRL-O earlier.

Figure 4-3. Bottom of Pico display while saving work

Managing Your Files

The tree structure of the Unix filesystem makes it easy to organize your files. After you make and edit some files, you may want to copy or move files from one directory to another, or rename files to distinguish different versions of a file. You may want to create new directories each time you start a different project.

A directory tree can get cluttered with old files you don't need. If you don't need a file or a directory, delete it to free storage space on the disk. The following sections explain how to make and remove directories and files.

Creating Directories with mkdir

It's handy to group related files in the same directory. If you were writing a spy novel, you probably wouldn't want your intriguing files mixed with restaurant listings. You could create two directories: one for all the chapters in your novel (*spy*, for example), and another for restaurants (*boston.dine*).

To create a new directory, use the **mkdir** program. The syntax is:

   mkdir *dirname(s)*

dirname is the name of the new directory. To make several directories, put a space between each directory name. To continue our example, you would enter:

```
$ mkdir spy boston.dine
```

Copying Files

If you're about to edit a file, you may want to save a copy first. That makes it easy to get back the original version.

cp

The **cp** program can put a copy of a file into the same directory or into another directory. **cp** doesn't affect the original file, so it's a good way to keep an identical backup of a file.

To copy a file, use the command:

    cp *old new*

where *old* is a pathname to the original file and *new* is the pathname you want for the copy. For example, to copy the */etc/passwd* file into a file called *password* in your working directory, you would enter:

```
$ cp /etc/passwd password
$
```

You can also use the form:

    cp *old olddir*

This puts a copy of the original file *old* into an existing directory *olddir*. The copy will have the same filename as the original.

If there's already a file with the same name as the copy, **cp** replaces the old file with your new copy. This is handy when you want to replace an old copy with a newer version, but it can cause trouble if you accidentally overwrite a copy you wanted to keep. To be safe, use **ls** to list the directory before you make a copy there. Also, many versions of **cp** have an –i (interactive) option that asks you before overwriting an existing file.

You can copy more than one file at a time to a single directory by listing the pathname of each file you want copied, with the destination directory at the end of the command line. You can use relative or absolute pathnames (see "the section "The Unix Filesystem" in Chapter 3) as well as simple filenames. For example, let's say your working directory is */users/carol* (from the filesystem diagram in Figure 3-1). To copy three files called *ch1*, *ch2*, and *ch3* from */users/john* to a subdirectory called *work* (that's */users/carol/work*), enter:

```
$ cp ../john/ch1 ../john/ch2 ../john/ch3 work
```

Or, you could use wildcards and let the shell find all the appropriate files. This time, let's add the –i option for safety:

```
$ cp -i ../john/ch[1-3] work
cp: overwrite work/ch2? n
```

There is already a file named *ch2* in the *work* directory. When **cp** asks, answer **n** to prevent copying *ch2*. Answering **y** would overwrite the old *ch2*.

As you saw in the section "Relative pathnames up" in Chapter 3, the shorthand form . puts the copy in the working directory, and .. puts it in the parent directory. For example, the following puts the copies into the working directory:

```
$ cp ../john/ch[1-3] .
```

cp can also copy entire directory trees. Use the option **-R**, for "recursive." There are two arguments after the option: the pathname of the top-level directory you want to copy from, and the pathname of the place where you want the top level of the copy to be. As an example, let's say that a new employee, Asha, has joined John and Carol. She needs a copy of John's *work* directory in her own home directory. See the filesystem diagram in Figure 3-1. Her home directory is */users/asha*. If Asha's own *work* directory doesn't exist yet (important!), she could type the following commands:

```
$ cd /users
$ cp -R john/work asha/work
```

Or, from her home directory, she could have typed "**cp -R ../john/work work**". Either way, she'd now have a new subdirectory */users/asha/work* with a copy of all files and subdirectories from */users/john/work*.

If you give **cp -R** the wrong pathnames, it can copy a directory tree into itself—running forever until your filesystem fills up!

If the copy seems to be taking a long time, stop **cp** with CTRL-Z , then explore the filesystem (**ls -RF** is handy for this). If all's okay, you can resume the copying by putting the **cp** job in the background (with **bg**) so it can finish its slow work. Otherwise, kill **cp** and do some cleanup— probably with **rm -r**, which we mention in the section "rmdir" later in this chapter. (See the section "Running a Command in the Background" and the section "Cancelling a Process" in Chapter 7.)

Problem checklist

The system says something like "cp: cannot copy file to itself."
> If the copy is in the same directory as the original, the filenames must be different.

The system says something like "cp: filename: no such file or directory."
> The system can't find the file you want to copy. Check for a typing mistake. If a file isn't in the working directory, be sure to use its pathname.

The system says something like "cp: permission denied."
> You may not have permission to copy a file created by someone else or copy it into a directory that does not belong to you. Use **ls -l** to find the owner and the permissions for the file, or **ls -ld** to check the directory. If you feel that you should be able to copy a file, ask the file's owner or a system staff person to change its access modes.

Copying files across a network

The **cp** program works on whatever computer you're logged onto. But, unless your computer has a networked filesystem (see the section "The Directory Tree" in Chapter 3), you can't copy files to other computers with **cp**. To do this, see the section "Transferring Files" in Chapter 6.

Renaming and Moving Files with mv

To rename a file, use **mv** (move). The **mv** program can also move a file from one directory to another.

The **mv** command has the same syntax as the **cp** command:

> mv *old new*

old is the old name of the file and *new* is the new name. **mv** will write over existing files, which is handy for updating old versions of a file. If you don't want to overwrite an old file, be sure that the new name is unique. If your **cp** has an **-i** option for safety, your **mv** probably has one too.

```
$ mv chap1 intro
$
```

The previous example changed the file named *chap1* to *intro*. If you list your files with **ls**, you will see that the filename *chap1* has disappeared.

The **mv** command can also move a file from one directory to another. As with the **cp** command, if you want to keep the same filename, you only need to give **mv** the name of the destination directory.

Finding Files

If your account has lots of files, organizing them into subdirectories can help you find the files later. Sometimes you may not remember which subdirectory has a file. The **find** program can search for files in many ways; we'll look at two.

Change to your home directory so **find** will start its search there. Then carefully enter one of the following two **find** commands. (The syntax is strange and ugly—but **find** does the job!)

```
$ cd
$ find . -type f -name "chap*" -print
./chap2
./old/chap10b
$ find . -type f -mtime -2 -print
./work/to_do
```

The first command looked in your working directory (.) and all its subdirectories for files (**-type f**) whose names start with *chap*. (**find** understands wildcards in filenames. Be sure to put quotes around any filename pattern with a wildcard in it, as we did in the example.) The second command looked for all files that have been created or modified in the last two days (**-mtime -2**). The relative pathnames that **find** finds start with a dot (./), the name of the working directory, which you can ignore.

Linux systems, and some others, have the GNU **locate** program. If it's been set up and maintained on your system, you can use **locate** to search part or all of a filesystem for a file with a certain name. For instance, if you're looking for a file named *alpha-test*, *alphatest*, or something like that, try this:

```
$ locate alpha
/users/alan/alpha3
/usr/local/projects/mega/alphatest
```

You'll get the absolute pathnames of files and directories with *alpha* in their names. (If you get a lot of output, add a pipe to **less**—see the section "Piping to a Pager" in Chapter 5.) **locate** may or may not list protected, private files; its listings usually also aren't completely up to date. To learn much more about **find** and **locate**, read your online documentation (see Chapter 8) or read the chapter about them in *Unix Power Tools* (O'Reilly).

Removing Files and Directories

You may have finished work on a file or directory and see no need to keep it, or the contents may be obsolete. Periodically removing unwanted files and directories frees storage space.

rm

The **rm** program removes files. The syntax is simple:

    rm *filename(s)*

rm removes the named files, as the following example shows:

```
$ ls
chap10        chap2      chap5    cold
chap1a.old    chap3.old  chap6    haha
chap1b        chap4      chap7    oldjunk
$ rm *.old chap10
$ ls
chap1b    chap4    chap6    cold    oldjunk
chap2     chap5    chap7    haha
$ rm c*
$ ls
haha      oldjunk
$
```

When you use wildcards with **rm**, be sure you're deleting the right files! If you accidentally remove a file you need, you can't recover it unless you have a copy in another directory or in the system backups.

Do not enter **rm *** carelessly. It deletes all the files in your working directory.

Here's another easy mistake to make: you want to enter a command such as **rm c*** (remove all filenames starting with "c") but instead enter **rm c *** (remove the file named **c** and all files!).

It's good practice to list the files with **ls** before you remove them. Or, if you use **rm**'s **-i** (*i*nteractive) option, **rm** asks you whether you want to remove each file.

---

rmdir

Just as you can create new directories, you can remove them with the **rmdir** program. As a precaution, **rmdir** won't let you delete directories that contain any files or subdirectories; the directory must first be empty. (The **rm -r** command removes a directory and everything in it. It can be dangerous for beginners, though.)

The syntax is:

> **rmdir** *dirname(s)*

If a directory you try to remove does contain files, you get a message like "rmdir: *dirname* not empty".

To delete a directory that contains some files:

1. Enter "**cd** *dirname*" to get into the directory you want to delete.

2. Enter "**rm** *" to remove all files in that directory.

3. Enter "**cd ..**" to go to the parent directory.

4. Enter "**rmdir** *dirname*" to remove the unwanted directory.

Problem checklist

I still get the message "dirname not empty" even after I've deleted all the files.

>   Use **ls -a** to check that there are no hidden files (names that start with a period) other than **.** and **..** (the working directory and its parent). The following command is good for cleaning up hidden files (which aren't matched by a simple wildcard like *):
>
> ```
> $ rm .[a-zA-Z] .??*
> ```

Files on Other Operating Systems

Chapter 6 includes the section "Transferring Files," which explains ways to transfer files across a network—possibly to nonUnix operating systems. Your system may also be able to run operating systems other than Unix. For instance, many Linux systems can also run Microsoft Windows. If yours does, you can probably use those files from your Linux account without needing to boot and run Windows.

If the Windows filesystem is *mounted* with your other filesystems, you'll be able to use its files by typing a Unix-like pathname. For instance, from our PC under Linux, we can access the Windows file *C:\WORD\REPORT.DOC* through the pathname */winc/word/report.doc*.

Your Linux (or other) system may also have the MTOOLS utilities. These give you Windows-like (actually, DOS-like) programs that interoperate with the Unix-like system. For example, we can put a Windows floppy disk in the A: drive and then copy a file named *summary.txt* into our current directory (.) by entering:

```
$ mcopy a:summary.txt .
Copying summary.txt
$
```

The **mcopy -t** option translates the end-of-line characters in plain-text files from the Windows format to the Unix format or vice versa. In general, *don't* use -t unless you're sure that you need to translate end-of-line characters. A local expert should be able to tell you about translation, whether other filesystems are mounted or can be mounted, whether you have utilities like MTOOLS, and how to use them.

Printing Files

Before you print a file on a Unix system, you may want to reformat it to adjust the margins, highlight some words, and so on. Most files can also be printed without reformatting, but the raw printout may not look quite as nice.

Many versions of Unix include two powerful text formatters, **nroff** and **troff**. (There are also versions called **gnroff** and **groff**.) They are much too complex to describe here. Before we cover printing itself, let's look at a simple formatting program called **pr**.

pr

The **pr** program does minor formatting of files on the terminal screen or for a printer. For example, if you have a long list of names in a file, you can format it onscreen into two or more columns.

The syntax is:

> **pr** *option(s) filename(s)*

pr changes the format of the file only on the screen or on the printed copy; it doesn't modify the original file. Table 4-1 lists some **pr** options.

Table 4-1. Some pr options

Option	Description
−k	Produces *k* columns of output.
−d	Double-spaces the output (not on all **pr** versions).
−h "*header*"	Takes the next item as a report *header*.
−t	Eliminates printing of header and top/bottom margins.

Other options allow you to specify the width of columns, set the page length, etc.

Before using **pr**, here are the contents of a sample file named *food*:

```
$ cat food
Sweet Tooth
Bangkok Wok
Mandalay
Afghani Cuisine
Isle of Java
Big Apple Deli
Sushi and Sashimi
Tio Pepe's Peppers
        .
        .
        .
```

Let's use **pr** options to make a two-column report with the header "Restaurants":

```
$ pr -2 -h "Restaurants" food

Oct  6  9:58 2001   Restaurants    Page 1

Sweet Tooth              Isle of Java
Bangkok Wok              Big Apple Deli
Mandalay                 Sushi and Sashimi
Afghani Cuisine          Tio Pepe's Peppers
        .
        .
        .
$
```

The text is output in two-column pages. The top of each page has the date and time, header (or name of the file, if header is not supplied), and page number. To send this output to the printer instead of the terminal screen, create a pipe to the printer program—usually **lp** or **lpr**. The following section describes **lp** and **lpr**; Chapter 5 covers pipes.

lp and lpr

The command **lp** or **lpr** prints a file (onto paper as opposed to the screen). Some systems have **lp**; others have **lpr**. The syntax is:

> lp *option(s) filename(s)*
> lpr *option(s) filename(s)*

Printers on Unix systems are usually shared by a group of users. After you enter the command to print a file, the shell prompt returns to the screen and you can enter another command. However, seeing the prompt doesn't mean that your file has been printed. Your file has been added to the printer queue to be printed in turn.

Your system administrator has probably set up a default printer at your site. To print a file named *bills* on the default printer, use the **lp** or **lpr** command, as in this example:

```
$ lp bills
request id is laserp-525  (1 file)
$
```

lp shows an ID that you can use to cancel the print job or check its status. If you need ID numbers for **lpr** jobs, use the **lpq** program (see the section "lpstat and lpq" later in this chapter). The file *bills* will be sent to a printer called *laserp*. The ID number of the request is "laserp-525."

lp and **lpr** have several options. Table 4-2 lists three of them.

Table 4-2. Some lp and lpr options

Option		
lp	lpr	Description
-d*printer*	-P*printer*	Use given *printer* name if there is more than one printer at your site. The printer names are assigned by the system administrator.
-n#	-#	Print # copies of the file.
-m	-m	Notify sender by email when printing is done.

Windowing applications like StarOffice typically run **lp** or **lpr** for you, "behind the scenes." They may have a printer configuration menu entry where you can specify any **lp** or **lpr** options you want to use on every print job.

If **lp** and **lpr** don't work at your site, ask other users for the printer command. You'll also need the printer locations, so you know where to get your output.

Problem checklist

My printout hasn't come out.

See whether the printer is printing now. If it is, other users may have made a request to the same printer ahead of you and your file should be printed in turn. The following section explains how to check the print requests.

If no file is printing, check the printer's paper supply, physical connections, and power switch. The printer may also be hung (stalled). If it is, ask other users or system staff people for advice.

My printout is garbled or doesn't look anything like the file did on my terminal.

The printer may not be configured to print the kind of file you're printing. For instance, a file in PostScript format will look fine when you use a PostScript viewer on your terminal, but look like gibberish when you try to print it. If the printer doesn't understand PostScript, ask your system administrator to install a printer driver that handles PostScript.

You may be trying to print a file directly (with **lp** or **lpr**) that should be printed from its own application. For instance, if you have a StarOffice file named *report.sdw*, you should open that file from a StarOffice window and use the Print command on the StarOffice File menu.

Viewing the Printer Queue

If you want to find out how many files or "requests" for output are ahead of yours in the printer queue, use the program named **lpstat** (for **lp**) or **lpq** (for **lpr**). The **cancel** program lets you terminate a printing request made by **lp**; **lprm** cancels jobs from **lpr**.

If you have a graphical application such as StarOffice that does its printing with **lp** or **lpr**, you should be able to use these commands to check and cancel those print jobs.

lpstat and lpq

The **lpstat** program shows what's in the printer queue: request IDs, owners, file sizes, when the jobs were sent for printing, and the status of the requests. Use **lpstat -o** if you want to see all output requests rather than just your own. Requests are shown in the order they'll be printed:

```
$ lpstat -o
laserp-573  john   128865  Oct 6  11:27  on laserp
laserp-574  grace  82744   Oct 6  11:28
laserp-575  john   23347   Oct 6  11:35
$
```

The first entry shows that the request "laserp-573" is currently printing on *laserp*. The exact format and amount of information given about the printer queue may differ from system to system. If the printer queue is empty, **lpstat** says "No entries" or simply gives you back the shell prompt.

lpq gives slightly different information than **lpstat -o**:

```
$ lpq
laserp is ready and printing
Rank    Owner     Job  Files                Total Size
active  john      573  report.ps            128865 bytes
1st     grace     574  ch03.ps ch04.ps      82744 bytes
2nd     john      575  standard input       23347 bytes
$
```

The first line displays the printer status. If the printer is disabled or out of paper, you may see different messages on this first line. The "active" job, the one being printed, is listed first. The "Job" number is like the **lpstat** request ID. To specify another printer, add the **-P** option (Table 4-2).

cancel and lprm

cancel terminates a printing request from the **lp** program. **lprm** terminates **lpr** requests. You can specify either the ID of the request (displayed by **lp** or **lpq**) or the name of the printer.

If you don't have the request ID, get it from **lpstat** or **lpq**. Then use **cancel** or **lprm**. Specifying the request ID cancels the request, even if it is currently printing:

```
$ cancel laserp-575
request "laserp-575" cancelled
```

To cancel whatever request is currently printing, regardless of its ID, simply enter **cancel** and the printer name:

```
$ cancel laserp
request "laserp-573" cancelled
```

The **lprm** program will cancel the active job if it belongs to you. Otherwise, you can give job numbers as arguments, or use a dash (–) to remove all of your jobs:

```
$ lprm 575
dfA575diamond dequeued
cfA575diamond dequeued
```

lprm tells you the actual filenames removed from the printer queue (which you probably don't need).

Exercise: manipulating files

In this exercise, you'll create, rename, and delete files. First you'll need to find out if your site has one or more printers and the appropriate command to use for printing.

Go to home directory.	Enter **cd**
Copy distant file to working directory.	Enter **cp /etc/passwd myfile**
Create new directory.	Enter **mkdir temp**
List working directory.	Enter **ls -F**
Move file to new directory.	Enter **mv myfile temp**
Change working directory.	Enter **cd temp**
Copy file to working directory.	Enter **cp myfile myfile.two**
Print the file.	Enter your printer command and the filename (if the file is long, you may want to edit it first—with Pico, for instance)
List filenames with wildcard.	Enter **ls -l myfile***
Remove files.	Enter **rm myfile***
Go up to parent directory.	Enter **cd ..**
Remove directory.	Enter **rmdir temp**
Verify that directory was removed.	Enter **ls -F**

5

Redirecting I/O

Many Unix programs read input (such as a file) and write output. In this chapter, we discuss Unix programs that handle their input and output in a standard way. This lets them work with each other.

This chapter generally *doesn't* apply to full-screen programs, such as the Pico editor, that take control of your whole terminal window. (The pager programs, **less**, **more**, and **pg**, *do* work together in this way.) It also doesn't apply to graphical programs, such as StarOffice or Netscape, that open their own windows on your screen.

Standard Input and Standard Output

What happens if you don't give a filename argument on a command line? Most programs will take their input from your keyboard instead (after you press the first RETURN to start the program running, that is). Your terminal keyboard is the program's *standard input.*

As a program runs, the results are usually displayed on your terminal screen. The terminal screen is the program's *standard output.*

So, by default, each of these programs takes its input from the standard input and sends the results to the standard output.

These two default cases of input/output (I/O) can be varied. This is called *I/O redirection.*

If a program doesn't normally read from files, but reads from its standard input, you can give a filename by using the < (less-than symbol) operator.

For example, the **mail** program (see the section "Sending Mail from a Shell Prompt" in Chapter 6) normally reads the message to send from your keyboard. Here's how to use the input redirection operator to mail the contents of the file *to_do* to *bigboss@corp.xyz*:

```
$ mail bigboss@corp.xyz < to_do
$
```

If a program writes to its standard output, which is normally the screen, you can make it write to a file instead by using the greater-than symbol (>) operator. The pipe operator (|) sends the standard output of one program to the standard input of another program. Input/output redirection is one of the most powerful and flexible Unix features, We'll take a closer look at it soon.

Putting Text in a File

Instead of always letting a program's output come to the screen, you can redirect output into a file. This is useful when you'd like to save program output or when you put files together to make a bigger file.

cat

cat, which is short for "concatenate," reads files and outputs their contents one after another, without stopping.

To display files on the standard output (your screen), use:

> cat *file(s)*

For example, let's display the contents of the file */etc/passwd*. This system file describes users' accounts. (Your system may have a more complete list somewhere else.)

```
$ cat /etc/passwd
root:x&k8KP30f;(:0:0:Root:/:
daemon:*:1:1:Admin:/:
       .
       .
       .
john::128:50:John Doe:/usr/john:/bin/sh
$
```

You cannot go back to view the previous screens, as you can when you use a pager program such as **less** (unless you're using a terminal window with a scrollbar, that is). **cat** is mainly used with redirection, as we'll see in a moment.

By the way: if you enter **cat** without a filename, it tries to read from the keyboard (as we mention earlier). You can get out by pressing RETURN followed by a single CTRL-D .

The > operator

When you add "> *filename*" to the end of a command line, the program's output is diverted from the standard output to the named file. The > symbol is called the *output redirection operator*.

When you use the > operator, be careful not to accidentally overwrite a file's contents. Your system may let you redirect output to an existing file. If so, the old file will be deleted (or, in Unix lingo, "clobbered"). Be careful not to overwrite a much needed file!

Many shells can protect you from this risk. In the C shell, use the command **set noclobber**. The Korn shell and **bash** command is **set –o noclobber**. Enter the command at a shell prompt or put it in your shell's startup file. After that, the shell does not allow you to redirect onto an existing file and overwrite its contents.

This doesn't protect against overwriting by Unix programs such as **cp**; it works only with the > redirection operator. For more protection, you can set Unix file access permissions.

For example, let's use **cat** with this operator. The file contents that you'd normally see on the screen (from the standard output) are diverted into another file, which we'll then read using **cat** (without any redirection!):

```
$ cat /etc/passwd > password
$ cat password
root:x&k8KP30f;(:0:0:Root:/:
daemon:*:1:1:Admin:/:
           .
           .
           .
john::128:50:John Doe:/usr/john:/bin/sh
$
```

An earlier example (in the section "cat") showed how **cat /etc/passwd** displays the file */etc/passwd* on the screen. The example here adds the >

operator; so the output of **cat** goes to a file called *password* in the working directory. Displaying the file *password* shows that its contents are the same as the file */etc/passwd* (the effect is the same as the copy command **cp /etc/passwd password**).

You can use the > redirection operator with any program that sends text to its standard output—not just with **cat**. For example:

```
$ who > users
$ date > today
$ ls
password   today   users   ...
```

We've sent the output of **who** to a file called *users* and the output of **date** to the file named *today*. Listing the directory shows the two new files. Let's look at the output from the **who** and **date** programs by reading these two files with **cat**:

```
$ cat users
tim     tty1    Aug 12   07:30
john    tty4    Aug 12   08:26
$ cat today
Tue Aug 12 08:36:09 EDT 2001
$
```

You can also use the **cat** program and the > operator to make a small text file. We told you earlier to type CTRL-D if you accidentally enter **cat** without a filename. This is because the **cat** program alone takes whatever you type on the keyboard as input. Thus, the command:

cat > *filename*

takes input from the keyboard and redirects it to a file. Try the following example:

```
$ cat > to_do
Finish report by noon
Lunch with Xannie
Swim at 5:30
^D
$
```

cat takes the text that you typed as input (in this example, the three lines that begin with **Finish**, **Lunch**, and **Swim**), and the > operator redirects it to a file called *to_do*. Type CTRL-D *once*, on a new line by itself, to signal the end of the text. You should get a shell prompt.

You can also create a bigger file from smaller files with the cat command and the > operator. The form:

cat *file1 file2* > *newfile*

creates a file *newfile*, consisting of *file1* followed by *file2*.

```
$ cat today to_do > diary
$ cat diary
Tue Aug 12 08:36:09 EDT 2001
Finish report by noon
Lunch with Xannie
Swim at 5:30
$
```

You can't use redirection to add a file to itself, along with other files. For example, you might hope that the following command would merge today's to-do list with tomorrow's. This won't work!

```
$ cat to_do to_do.tomorrow > to_do.tomorrow
cat: to_do.tomorrow: input file is output file
```

cat warns you, but it's actually already too late. When you redirect a program's output to a file, Unix empties (clobbers) the file *before* the program starts running. The right way to do this is by using a temporary file (as you'll see in a later example) or simply by using a text editor program.

The >> operator

You can add more text to the end of an existing file, instead of replacing its contents, by using the >> (append redirection) operator. Use it as you would the > (output redirection) operator. So:

cat *file2* >> *file1*

appends the contents of *file2* to the end of *file1*. For an example, let's append the contents of the file *users*, and also the current date and time, to the file *diary*. Then we display the file:

```
$ cat users >> diary
$ date >> diary
$ cat diary
Tue Aug 12 08:36:09 EDT 2001
```

```
Finish report by noon
Lunch with Xannie
Swim at 5:30
tim      tty1      Aug 12   07:30
john     tty4      Aug 12   08:26
Tue Aug 12 09:07:24 EDT 2001
$
```

Unix doesn't have a redirection operator that adds text to the beginning of a file. You can do this by storing the new text in a temporary file, then by using a text editor program to read the temporary file into the start of the file you want to edit. You also can do the job with a temporary file and redirection. Maybe you'd like each day's entry to go at the beginning of your *diary* file. Simply rename *diary* to something like *temp*. Make a new *diary* file with today's entries, then append *temp* (with its old contents) to the new *diary*. For example:*

```
$ mv diary temp
$ date > diary
$ cat users >> diary
$ cat temp >> diary
$ rm temp
```

Pipes and Filters

We've seen how to redirect input from a file and output to a file. You can also connect two *programs* together so that the output from one program becomes the input of the next program. Two or more programs connected in this way form a *pipe*. To make a pipe, put a vertical bar (|) on the command line between two commands. When a pipe is set up between two commands, the standard output of the command to the left of the pipe symbol becomes the standard input of the command to the right of the pipe symbol. Any two commands can form a pipe as long as the first program writes to standard output and the second program reads from standard input.

When a program takes its input from another program, performs some operation on that input, and writes the result to the standard output (which may be piped to yet another program), it is referred to as a *filter*. A common use of filters is to modify output. Just as a common filter culls unwanted items, Unix filters can restructure output.

---

* This example could be shortened by combining the two **cat** commands into one, giving both filenames as arguments to a single **cat** command. That wouldn't work, though, if you were making a real diary with a command other than **cat users**.

Most Unix programs can be used to form pipes. Some programs that are commonly used as filters are described in the next sections. Note that these programs aren't used only as filters or parts of pipes. They're also useful on their own.

grep

The **grep** program searches a file or files for lines that have a certain pattern. The syntax is:

> **grep** *"pattern" file(s)*

The name "grep" derives from the **ed** (a Unix line editor) command **g/re/p**, which means "*g*lobally search for a *r*egular *e*xpression and *p*rint all lines containing it." A *regular expression* is either some plain text (a word, for example) and/or special characters used for pattern matching. When you learn more about regular expressions, you can use them to specify complex patterns of text.

The simplest use of **grep** is to look for a pattern consisting of a single word. It can be used in a pipe so that only those lines of the input files containing a given string are sent to the standard output. But let's start with an example reading from files: searching all files in the working directory for a word—say, *Unix*. We'll use the wildcard * to quickly give **grep** all filenames in the directory.

```
$ grep "Unix" *
ch01:Unix is a flexible and powerful operating system
ch01:When the Unix designers started work, little did
ch05:What can we do with Unix?
$
```

When **grep** searches multiple files, it shows the filename where it finds each matching line of text. Alternatively, if you don't give **grep** a filename to read, it reads its standard input; that's the way all filter programs work:

```
$ ls -l | grep "Aug"
-rw-rw-rw-  1 john   doc    11008 Aug  6 14:10 ch02
-rw-rw-rw-  1 john   doc     8515 Aug  6 15:30 ch07
-rw-rw-r--  1 john   doc     2488 Aug 15 10:51 intro
-rw-rw-r--  1 carol  doc     1605 Aug 23 07:35 macros
$
```

First, the example runs **ls -l** to list your directory. The standard output of **ls -l** is piped to **grep**, which only outputs lines that contain the string *Aug* (that is, files that were last modified in August). Because the standard output of **grep** isn't redirected, those lines go to the terminal screen.

grep options let you modify the search. Table 5-1 lists some of the options.

Table 5-1. Some grep options

Option	Description
-v	Print all lines that do not match pattern.
-n	Print the matched line and its line number.
-l	Print only the names of files with matching lines (lowercase letter "L").
-c	Print only the count of matching lines.
-i	Match either upper- or lowercase.

Next, let's use a regular expression that tells **grep** to find lines with *carol,* followed by zero or more other characters (abbreviated in a regular expression as ".*"),* then followed by *Aug*:

```
$ ls -l | grep "carol.*Aug"
-rw-rw-r--   1 carol doc      1605 Aug 23 07:35 macros
$
```

For more about regular expressions, see the references in the section "Documentation" (Chapter 8).

sort

The **sort** program arranges lines of text alphabetically or numerically. The following example sorts the lines in the *food* file (from the section "Printing Files" in Chapter 4) alphabetically. **sort** doesn't modify the file itself; it reads the file and writes the sorted text to the standard output.

```
$ sort food
Afghani Cuisine
Bangkok Wok
Big Apple Deli
Isle of Java
Mandalay
Sushi and Sashimi
Sweet Tooth
Tio Pepe's Peppers
```

---

* Note that the regular expression for "zero or more characters," ".*", is different than the corresponding filename wildcard "*". See the section "File and Directory Wildcards" in Chapter 4. We can't cover regular expressions in enough depth here to explain the difference—though more-detailed books do. As a rule of thumb, remember that the first argument to **grep** is a regular expression; other arguments, if any, are filenames that can use wildcards.

By default, **sort** arranges lines of text alphabetically. Many options control the sorting, and Table 5-2 lists some of them.

Table 5-2. Some sort options

Option	Description
-n	Sort numerically (example: 10 sorts after 2), ignore blanks and tabs.
-r	Reverse the sorting order.
-f	Sort upper- and lowercase together.
+x	Ignore first x fields when sorting.

More than two commands may be linked up into a pipe. Taking a previous pipe example using **grep**, we can further sort the files modified in August by order of size. The following pipe uses the commands **ls**, **grep**, and **sort**:

```
$ ls -l | grep "Aug" | sort +4n
-rw-rw-r--  1 carol  doc     1605 Aug 23 07:35 macros
-rw-rw-r--  1 john   doc     2488 Aug 15 10:51 intro
-rw-rw-rw-  1 john   doc     8515 Aug  6 15:30 ch07
-rw-rw-rw-  1 john   doc    11008 Aug  6 14:10 ch02
$
```

This pipe sorts all files in your directory modified in August by order of size, and prints them to the terminal screen. The **sort** option **+4n** skips four fields (fields are separated by blanks), then sorts the lines in numeric order. So, the output of **ls**, filtered by **grep**, is sorted by the file size (this is the fifth column, starting with 1605). Both **grep** and **sort** are used here as filters to modify the output of the **ls -l** command. If you wanted to email this listing to someone, you could add a final pipe to the **mail** program. Or you could print the listing by piping the **sort** output to your printer command (either **lp** or **lpr**).

Piping to a Pager

The **less** program, which you saw in the section "Looking Inside Files with less" in Chapter 3, can also be used as a filter. A long output normally zips by you on the screen, but if you run text through **less**, the display stops after each screenful of text.

Let's assume that you have a long directory listing. (If you want to try this example and need a directory with lots of files, use **cd** first to change to a

system directory such as */bin* or */usr/bin*.) To make it easier to read the
sorted listing, pipe the output through **less**:

```
$ ls -l | grep "Aug" | sort +4n | less
-rw-rw-r-- 1 carol doc      1605 Aug 23 07:35 macros
-rw-rw-r-- 1 john  doc      2488 Aug 15 10:51 intro
-rw-rw-rw- 1 john  doc      8515 Aug  6 15:30 ch07
-rw-rw-r-- 1 john  doc     14827 Aug  9 12:40 ch03
           .
           .
           .
-rw-rw-rw- 1 john  doc     16867 Aug  6 15:56 ch05
:
```

less reads a screenful of text from the pipe (consisting of lines sorted by
order of file size), then prints a colon (:) prompt. At the prompt, you can
type a **less** command to move through the sorted text. **less** reads more text
from the pipe and shows it to you, as well as saves a copy of what it has
read, so you can go backwards to reread previous text if you want to.
(The simpler pager programs **more** and **pg** generally can't back up while
reading from a pipe.) When you're done seeing the sorted text, the **q**
command quits **less**.

Exercise: redirecting input/output

In the following exercises you redirect output, create a simple pipe, and
use filters to modify output.

Redirect output to a file.	Enter **who > users**
Email that file to yourself. (Replace *username* with your own username.)	Enter **mail** *username* **< users**
Sort output of a program.	Enter **who	sort**
Append sorted output to a file.	Enter **who	sort >> users**
Display output to screen.	Enter **less users** (or **more users** or **pg users**)
Display long output to screen.	Enter **ls -l /bin	less** (or **more** or **pg**)
Format and print a file with **pr**.	Enter **pr users	lp** or **pr users	lpr**

6

Using the Internet and Other Networks

A network lets computers communicate with each other, sharing files, email, and much more. Unix systems have been networked for more than 25 years.

This chapter introduces Unix networking: running programs on other computers, copying files between computers, browsing the World Wide Web, sending and receiving email messages, reading and posting messages to Usenet "Net news" discussions, and "chatting" interactively with other users on your local computer or worldwide.

Remote Logins

The computer you log in to may not be the computer you need to use. For instance, you might have a workstation on your desk but need to do some work on the main computer in another building. Or you might be a professor doing research with a computer at another university. Your Unix system can connect to another computer to let you work as if you were sitting at that computer. This section describes how to connect to another computer from a local terminal. If you need to use a graphical (nonterminal) program, the section "Windows from Other Computers," next, explains.

To log into a remote computer using a terminal, first log in to your local computer (as explained in the section "Logging in Nongraphically" in Chapter 1, or in the section "A. Ready to Run X (with a Graphical Login)" in Chapter 2). Then, in a terminal or terminal window on your local computer, start a program that connects to the remote computer. Some typical programs for connecting over a computer network are **telnet**, **ssh** ("secure shell"), **rsh**, ("remote shell") or **rlogin** ("remote login"). Programs such as **cu** and **tip** connect through telephone lines using a modem. In any case, when you log off the remote computer, the remote login program quits and you get another shell prompt from your local computer.

Figure 6-1 shows how remote login programs such as **telnet** work. In a local login, you interact directly with the shell program running on your local system. In a remote login, you run a remote-access program on your local system; that program lets you interact with a shell program on the remote system.

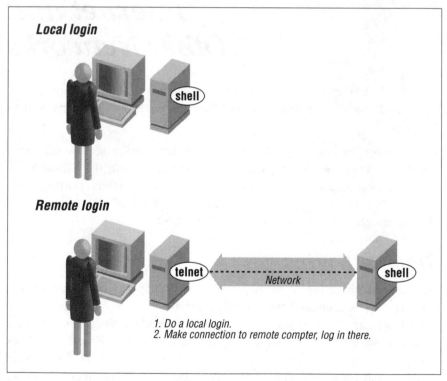

Figure 6-1. Local login, remote login

The syntax for most remote login programs is:

program-name remote-hostname

For example, when Dr. Nelson wants to connect to the remote computer named *biolab.medu.edu*, she'd first make a local login to her computer named *fuzzy*. Next, she'd use the **telnet** program to reach the remote computer. Her session would look something like this:

```
login: jennifer
Password:

NOTICE to all second-floor MDs: meeting in room 304 at 4 PM.

fuzzy$ telnet biolab.medu.edu

Medical University Biology Laboratory

biolab.medu.edu login: jdnelson
Password:

biolab$
        .
        .
        .
biolab$ exit
Connection closed by foreign host.
fuzzy$
```

Her accounts have shell prompts that include the hostname. This reminds her when she's logged in remotely. If you use more than one system but don't have the hostname in your prompt, see the section "Documentation" in Chapter 8 to find out how to add it.

When you're logged on to a remote system, keep in mind that the commands you type will take effect on the remote system, not your local one! For instance, if you use **lpr** or **lp** to print a file, the printer it comes out of may be very far away.

The programs **rsh** (also called **rlogin**) and **ssh** generally don't give you a "login:" prompt. These programs assume that your remote username is the same as your local username. If they're different, give your remote username on the command line of the remote login program, as shown in the next example.

You may be able to log in without typing your remote password or passphrase.* Otherwise, you'll be prompted after entering the command line.

---

* In **ssh**, you can run an *agent* program, such as **ssh-agent**, that asks for your passphrase once, and then handles authentication every time you run **ssh** or **scp** afterward. For **rsh** and **rcp**, you can either store your remote password in a file named *.rhosts* in your local home directory, or the remote system can list your local computer in a file named *hosts.equiv* that's set up by the system administrator.

Following are four sample **ssh** and **rsh** command lines. (You may need to substitute **rlogin** for **rsh**.) The first pair show the way to log in to the remote system, *biolab.medu.edu*, when your username is the same on both the local and remote systems. The second pair show how to log in if your remote username is different (in this case, *jdnelson*); note that your version of **ssh** and **rsh** may support both syntaxes shown:

```
$ ssh biolab.medu.edu
$ rsh biolab.medu.edu
$ ssh jdnelson@biolab.medu.edu
$ rsh -l jdnelson biolab.medu.edu
```

About Security

Today's Internet, and other public networks, have users (called *crackers*; also erroneously called *hackers*) who try to break into computers and snoop on other network users. Most remote login programs (and file transfer programs, which we cover later in this chapter) were designed 20 years ago or more, when networks were friendly places with cooperative users. Those programs (many versions of **telnet** and **rsh**, for instance) make a cracker's job easy. They transmit your data across the network in a way that allows crackers to read it—and they either send your password along, visible to the crackers, or they expect computers to allow access without passwords.

SSH is different; it was designed with security in mind. If anything you do over a network (like the Internet) is at all confidential, you really should find SSH programs and learn how to use them. SSH isn't just for Unix systems! There are SSH programs that let you log in and transfer files between Microsoft Windows machines, between Windows and Unix, and more. A good place to get all the details and recommendations for programs is the book *SSH: The Secure Shell*, by Daniel J. Barrett and Richard Silverman (O'Reilly).

Windows from Other Computers

In the section "Remote Logins," you saw how to open a terminal session across a network. The X Window System lets you ask a remote computer to open any kind of X window (not just a plain terminal) on your local system. This is hard or impossible to do with remote login programs such as *telnet*. It's also insecure over a public network such as the Internet.

The **ssh** program, when you use it together with an *SSH agent* program, can open remote windows securely and fairly easily, and without needing to log into the remote computer first. This is called *X forwarding*.

 Please show this section to your system or network administrator and ask for advice. Although SSH is secure, X forwarding can be resource-intensive, and the first-time setup can take some work. (Also, this concept may be new to your administrator, or he may just want to be aware of what you're doing.)

For example, let's say Dr. Nelson has a graphical data-analysis program named **datavis** on the remote *biolab.medu.edu* computer. She needs to run it from her local *fuzzy* computer. She could type a command like the following, and (if the first-time setup has been done) a **datavis** window will open on her local system. The connection will be encrypted for security, so no one else can see her data or anything she does to it:

```
fuzzy$ ssh jdnelson@biolab.medu.edu datavis
```

Figure 6-2 shows how this works when the **xterm** program runs on your local computer versus when **ssh** coordinates access to the remote **datavis** program.

Lynx, a Text-based Web Browser

In a window system, you can choose from lots of graphical web browsers: Netscape, Opera, KDE's Konqueror, the browser in StarOffice, and more. If you have a window system, try the various Unix browsers to find one you like. Those browsers don't work without a window system, though. They also can be slow—especially with flashy, graphics-laden web pages on a slow network.

The Lynx web browser (originally from the University of Kansas, and available on many Unix systems) is different, and has tradeoffs you should know about. It works in terminals (where graphical browsers can't) as well as in terminal windows. Lynx indicates where graphics occur in a page layout; you won't see the graphics, but the bits of text that Lynx uses in their place can clutter the screen. Still, because it doesn't have to download or display those graphics, Lynx is *fast*, especially over a dialup modem or busy network connection. Sites with complex multicolumn layouts can be hard to follow with Lynx; a good rule is to just page through

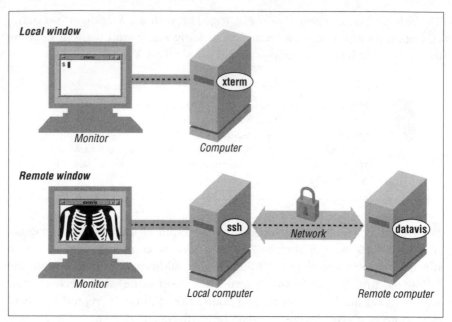

Figure 6-2. Local window, remote window

the screens, looking for the link you want and ignoring the rest. Forms and drop-down lists are a challenge at first—but Lynx always gives you helpful hints for forms and lists, as well as other web page elements, in the third line from the bottom of the screen. With those warts (and others), though, once you get a feel for Lynx you may find yourself choosing to use it—even on a graphical system. Let's take a quick tour.

The Lynx command line syntax is:

> **lynx** "*location*"

For example, to visit the O'Reilly home page, enter **lynx** "http://www.oreilly.com" or simply **lynx** "www.oreilly.com". (It's safest to put quotes around the location because many URLs have special characters that the shell might interpret otherwise.) Figure 6-3 shows a part of the home page.

To move around the Web, Lynx uses your keyboard's arrow keys, space bar, and a set of single-letter commands. The third line from the bottom of a Lynx screen gives you a hint of what you might want to do at the moment. In Figure 6-3, for instance, "press space for next page" means you can see the next screenful of this web page by pressing the space bar (at the bottom edge of your keyboard). Lynx doesn't use a scroll bar; instead, use the space bar to go forward in a page, and use the **b** command to move back to the previous screenful of the same web page. The bottom two lines of the screen remind you of common commands, and the help system (which you get by typing **h**) has the rest.

```
www.oreilly.com -- Welcome to O'Reilly & Associates    (p8 of 14)

Essential SNMP --This guide for network and system administrators
   introduces SNMP, an Internet-standard protocol for managing
   hosts on an IP network. The book's primary focus is on
   network administration. Essential SNMP covers all versions
   through SNMPv3, and it also explores commercial and open source
   packages, including OpenView, SNMPc, and MRTG. Sample Chapter 2,
   A Closer Look at SNMP, is available online.

   Dreamweaver 4: The Missing Manual is a complete user's guide
   to Macromedia Dreamweaver. This Missing Manual also
   shows how to customize Dreamweaver with libraries, templates,
   shortcuts, and extensions. Sample Chapter 17, Libraries and
   Templates, is available online in PDF format.

-- press space for next page --
   Up and Down keys move.  Right follows a link; Left goes back.
   H)elp O)ptions P)rint G)o Q)uit /=search [delete]=history list
```

Figure 6-3. Lynx display

The links (which you would click on if you were using a graphical web browser) are highlighted. One of those links is the *currently selected link*, which you can think of as the link where your cursor sits. On a monochrome terminal, links are boldfaced and the selected link (in Figure 6-3, that's the first "Essential SNMP") is in reverse video. Emphasized text is also boldfaced on monochrome terminals, but you won't be able to select it as you move through the links on the page. On a color terminal, links are blue, the selected link is red, and emphasized text is pink.

When you first view a screen, the link nearest the top is selected. Figure 6-4 shows what you can do at a selected link. To select a later link (farther down the page), press the down-arrow key. The up-arrow key selects the previous link (farther up the page). Once you've selected a link you want to visit, press the right-arrow key to follow that link; the new page appears. Go back to the previous page by pressing the left-arrow key (from any selected link; it doesn't matter which one).

Although Lynx can't display graphics in a terminal (*no* program can!), it will let you download links that point to graphical files—such as the last link in Figure 6-3, for instance, Then you can use other Unix programs—such as **gimp** or **xv** (for graphics), and **acroread** (for PDF documents)—to view or print those files.

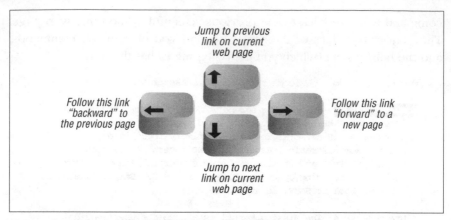

Figure 6-4. Lynx link navigation with the arrow keys

There's much more to Lynx; type H for an overview. Lynx command-line options let you configure almost everything. For a list of options, type **man lynx** (see the section "Documentation" in Chapter 8) or use:

```
$ lynx -help | less
```

Transferring Files

You may need to copy files between computers. For instance, you can put a backup copy of an important file you're editing onto an account at a computer in another building, or another city. Dr. Nelson could put a copy of a data file from her local computer onto a central computer, where her colleagues can access it. Or you might want to download 20 files from an FTP server, but not want to go through the tedious process of clicking on them one-by-one in a web browser window. If you need to do this sort of thing often, your system administrator may be able to set up a networked filesystem connection; then you'll be able to use local programs such as **cp** and **mv**. But Unix systems also have command-line tools for transferring files between computers. These often do it more quickly than working with graphical tools does. We explore them later in this section.

scp and rcp

Your system may have an **scp** (secure copy) or **rcp** (remote copy) program for copying files between two computers. In general, you must have accounts on both computers to use these. The syntax of **scp** and **rcp** are like **cp**, but also let you add the remote hostname to the start of a file or directory pathname. The syntax of each argument is:

   hostname:pathname

hostname: is needed only for remote files. You can copy from a remote computer to the local computer, from the local computer to a remote computer, or between two remote computers.

The **scp** program is much more secure than **rcp**, so we suggest using **scp** to transfer private files over insecure networks such as the Internet. For privacy, **scp** encrypts the file and your passphrase.

For example, let's copy the files named *report.may* and *report.june* from your home directory on the computer named *giraffe* and put the copies into your working directory (.) on the machine you're logged in to now. If you haven't set up the SSH agent that lets you use **scp** without typing your passphrase, **scp** will ask you:

```
$ scp giraffe:report.may giraffe:report.june .
Enter passphrase for RSA key 'jpeek@home':
```

To use wildcards in the remote filenames, put quotation marks (*"name"*) around each remote name.* You can use absolute or relative pathnames; if you use relative pathnames, they start from your home directory on the remote system. For example, to copy all files from your *food/lunch* subdirectory on your *giraffe* account into your working directory (.) on the local account, enter:

```
$ scp "giraffe:food/lunch/*" .
```

Unlike **cp**, most versions of **scp** and **rcp** don't have an **-i** safety option. If the files you're copying already exist on the destination system (in the previous example, that's your local machine), those files are overwritten.

If your system has **rcp**, your system administrator may not want you to use it for system security reasons. Another program, **ftp**, is more flexible and secure than **rcp** (but much *less* secure than **scp**).

FTP

FTP, file transfer protocol, is a standard way to transfer files between two computers. The Unix **ftp** program does FTP transfers from the command line.† (Your system may have a friendlier version of **ftp** named **ncftp**. Some graphical filesystem browsers can also handle FTP transfers. But we

---

* Quotes tell the local shell not to interpret special characters, such as wildcards, in the filename. The wildcards are passed, unquoted, to the remote shell, which interprets them *there*.

† Microsoft Windows, and some other operating systems, have a version of **ftp** that you can use from a command prompt. It works just like the Unix version.

cover the standard **ftp** program here.) Both computers must be connected by a network (such as the Internet), but they don't need to run Unix.

To start FTP, identify yourself to the remote computer by giving the username and password for your account on that remote system. Unfortunately, sending your username and password over a public network means that snoopers may see them—and use them to log into your account on that system.

A special kind of FTP, *anonymous FTP*, happens if you log into the remote server with the username *anonymous*. The password is your email address, like *alex@foo.co.uk*. (The password usually isn't required; it's a courtesy to the remote server.) Anonymous FTP lets anyone log into a remote system and download publicly-accessible files to their local systems.

Command-line ftp

To start the standard Unix **ftp** program, provide the remote computer's hostname:

> **ftp** *hostname*

ftp prompts for your username and password on the remote computer. This is something like a remote login (see the section "Remote Logins," earlier in this chapter), but **ftp** doesn't start your usual shell. Instead, **ftp** prints its own prompt and uses a special set of commands for transferring files. Table 6-1 lists the most important **ftp** commands.

Table 6-1. Some ftp commands

Command	Description
put *filename*	Copies the file *filename* from your local computer to the remote computer. If you give a second argument, the remote copy will have that name.
mput *filenames*	Copies the named files (you can use wildcards) from local to remote.
get *filename*	Copies the file *filename* from the remote computer to your local computer. If you give a second argument, the local copy will have that name.
mget *filenames*	Copies the named files (you can use wildcards) from remote to local.

Table 6-1. Some ftp commands (continued)

Command	Description
prompt •	A "toggle" command that turns prompting on or off during transfers with the **mget** and **mput** commands. By default, **mget** and **mput** will prompt you "mget *filename*?" or "mput *filename*?" before transferring each file; you answer *y* or *n* each time. Typing **prompt** once, from an "ftp>" prompt, stops the prompting: all files will be transferred without question until the end of the **ftp** session. Or, if prompting is off, typing **prompt** at an "ftp>" prompt resumes prompting.
cd *pathname*	Changes the working directory on the remote machine to *pathname* (**ftp** typically starts at your home directory on the remote machine).
lcd *pathname*	Changes **ftp**'s working directory on the local machine to *pathname*. (**ftp**'s first local working directory is the same working directory from which you started the program.) Note that the **ftp** lcd command changes only **ftp**'s working directory. After you quit **ftp**, your shell's working directory will not have changed.
dir	Lists the remote directory (like **ls -l**).
binary	Tells **ftp** to copy the following file(s) without translation. This preserves pictures, sound, or other data.
ascii	Transfers plain text files, translating data if needed. For instance, during transfers between a Microsoft Windows system (which adds CTRL-M to the end of each line of text) and a Unix system (which doesn't), an **ascii**-mode transfer removes or adds those characters as needed.
quit	Ends the **ftp** session and takes you back to a shell prompt.

Here's an example. Carol uses **ftp** to copy the file *todo* from her *work* sub-directory on her account on the remote computer *rhino*:

```
$ ls
afile    ch2     somefile
$ ftp rhino
Connected to rhino.zoo.edu.
Name (rhino:carol): csmith
Password:
ftp> cd work
ftp> dir
total 3
-rw-r--r--  1 csmith    mgmt      47 Feb  5  2001 for.ed
-rw-r--r--  1 csmith    mgmt     264 Oct 11 12:18 message
-rw-r--r--  1 csmith    mgmt     724 Nov 20 14:53 todo
ftp> get todo
```

```
ftp> quit
$ ls
afile    ch2    somefile    todo
```

We've explored the most basic **ftp** commands here. Entering **help** at an ftp> prompt gives a list of all commands; entering **help** followed by an **ftp** command name gives a one-line summary of that command.

FTP with a web browser

If you need a file from a remote site, and you don't need all the control that you get with the **ftp** program, you can use a web browser to download files using anonymous FTP. To do that, make a URL (location) with this syntax:

> ftp://*hostname*/*pathname*

For instance, *ftp://somecorp.za/pub/reports/2001.pdf* specifies the file *2001.pdf* from the directory */pub/reports* on the host *somecorp.za*. In most cases, you can also start with just the first part of the URL—such as *ftp://somecorp.za*—and browse your way through the FTP directory tree to find what you want. If your web browser doesn't prompt you to save a file, use its "Save" menu command.

An even faster way to download a file is with the handy Lynx web browser. Its **-dump** option sends a page to the standard output, where you can redirect it to a file or pipe it to another program (see Chapter 5). For example, to save the report in a file named *report.pdf*, enter:

```
$ lynx -dump "ftp://somecorp.za/pub/reports/2001.pdf" > report.pdf
```

Electronic Mail

You may see a notice that says "You have mail" when you first log in to your system, or later, before a shell prompt. Someone has sent you a message or document by *electronic mail* (email). With email, you can compose a message at your terminal and send it to another user or list of users. You also can read any messages that others may have sent to you.

There are a lot of email programs for Unix. If you'll use email often, we recommend that you start with whatever program other people in your group use.

We start with a brief section on addressing email. Next, you'll see how to send mail from a shell prompt with Berkeley **mail**. Then we introduce sending and reading mail with Pine, a popular menu-driven program that works without a window system. If you'd like to try a graphical program (which we won't discuss here), many web browsers have an email window. All programs' basic principles are the same though, and they all can send and receive messages from each other.*

Addressing an Email Message

Most addresses have this syntax:

> *username@hostname*

username is the person's username, like *jerry*, and *hostname* is either the name of his computer or a central domain name for his entire organization, like *oreilly.com*. On many Unix systems, if the recipient reads email on the same computer you do, you may omit the *@hostname*. (An easy way to get a copy of a message you send is to add your username to the list of addressees.)

Sending Mail from a Shell Prompt

Most Unix systems have a fairly simple program from Berkeley Unix called **Mail** (with an uppercase "M"), **mailx**, or just **mail**. If you enter just the program name at a shell prompt, you can read your email, but its terse interface isn't very friendly. If you enter the program name, followed by addresses as arguments, you can send an email message. This is handy for sending a quick message from your keyboard. But it's best used with redirection (explained in Chapter 5) to email the output of a program or the contents of a file.

To send mail, give the address of each person you want to send a message to, such as one of the following:

> **Mail** *address1 address2* ...
>
> **mailx** *address1 address2* ...
>
> **mail** *address1 address2* ...

---

* Microsoft Windows users have an unfortunate habit of sending email "attachments" made with a Windows-specific program like Microsoft Word. On Unix systems, you can read these messages using popular word processing programs such as StarOffice, but it can be a pain. You might ask Windows users to send plain text messages, which everyone can read without special software.

It's best to use simple addresses such as *username@host-name* on the command line. More complex addresses— with peoples' names or special characters such as < and >—can cause trouble unless you know how to deal with them.

After you enter **mail** and the addresses, if you're sending a message from the keyboard, in most cases the program (depending on how it's set up) prompts you for the subject of the message. Many versions of the program also accept a subject as a command-line argument after the **-s** option; be sure to put quote marks around the subject! Here are two examples of redirection: first sending the restaurant list you made in an earlier example, then sorting the list before you send it:

```
$ mail -s "My favorite restaurants" jerry@oreilly.com < food
$ sort food | mail -s "My favorite restaurants" jerry@oreilly.com
```

If you've redirected the standard input from a pipe or file, as in these two examples, your message will be delivered. Otherwise, *mail* will wait for you to enter the message body. Type in your message, line by line, pressing RETURN after every line. When you've finished entering text, type CTRL-D (just once!) at the start of a new line. You should get the shell prompt at this point, though it might take a few seconds.

```
$ mail alicja@moxco.chi.il.us
Subject: My Chicago trip
Alicja, I will be able to attend your meeting.
Please send me the agenda. Thanks.

Jerry
^D
$
```

If you change your mind before you type CTRL-D , you can cancel a message (while you're still entering text) with your interrupt character (see the section "Correcting a Command Line" in Chapter 1). The cancelled message may be placed in a file called *dead.letter* in your home directory. To see other commands you can use while sending mail, enter ~? (tilde question mark) at the start of a line of your message, then press RETURN . To redisplay your message after using ~?, enter ~p at the start of a line.

You can't cancel a message after you type CTRL-D (unless you're a system administrator and you're lucky to catch the message in time). So, if you change your mind about Alicja's meeting, you'll need to send her another message.

Please try the previous examples, substituting your address for the sample addresses shown. Once you've found the correct program name and the email address you can use to send a message to yourself, write them down. You'll probably find this is a very useful way to send yourself little reminder messages, the contents of files, and the outputs of programs:

_____ Name of email program that sends from a shell prompt

_____ My email address

Reading Email with Pine

Pine, from the University of Washington, is a popular program for reading and sending email from a terminal. It works completely from your keyboard; you don't need a mouse. Pine isn't a standard part of all Unix systems; if you don't have it, you can use other email programs. If you read this introduction but don't have Pine, ask your system staff to download and install it. Like most Unix software, Pine is free.

Start Pine by entering its name at a shell prompt. It also accepts options and arguments on its command line; to find out more, enter **pine -h** ("help"). If new email is waiting for you, but you want to experiment with Pine without taking chances, the –o (lowercase letter "O") option makes your inbox folder read-only; you won't be able to change the messages in it until you quit Pine and restart without the -o. Figure 6-5 shows the starting display, the *main menu.*

The highlighted line, which is the default command, gives a list of your email folders.* You can choose the highlighted command by pressing RETURN , pressing the greater-than sign >, or typing the letter next to it (here, l, a lowercase L; you don't need to type the commands in uppercase). But since you probably haven't used Pine before, the only interesting folder is the inbox, which is the folder where your new messages wait for you to read them.

---

* Recent versions of Pine also let you read Usenet newsgroups. The L command takes you to another display where you choose the source of the folders, *then* you see the list of folders from that source. See the section "Usenet News," later in this chapter.

```
PINE 4.33    MAIN MENU                          Folder: INBOX   2 Messages

      ?    HELP                - Get help using Pine

      C    COMPOSE MESSAGE     - Compose and send/post a message

      I    MESSAGE INDEX       - View messages in current folder

      L    FOLDER LIST         - Select a folder OR news group to view

      A    ADDRESS BOOK        - Update address book

      S    SETUP               - Configure Pine Options

      Q    QUIT                - Leave the Pine program

   Copyright 1989-2001.
   PINE is a trademark of the University of Washington.
               [Folder "INBOX" opened with 2 messages]
? Help                          P To Files    R RelNotes
O OTHER CMDS  > [ListFldrs]     N NextCmd     K KBlock
```

Figure 6-5. Pine main menu

The bottom of the display in Figure 6-5 shows that there are two messages waiting. Let's go directly to the inbox by pressing $\boxed{\text{I}}$ (or by highlighting that line in the menu and pressing $\boxed{\text{RETURN}}$) to read the new mail. Figure 6-6 has the *message index* for Alicja's inbox.

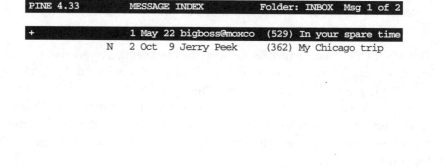

```
PINE 4.33         MESSAGE INDEX        Folder: INBOX  Msg 1 of 2

+                     1 May 22 bigboss@moxco  (529) In your spare time
                    N 2 Oct  9 Jerry Peek      (362) My Chicago trip
```

```
? Help       < FldrList P PrevMsg  - PrevPage D Delete   R Reply
O OTHER CMDS > [ViewMsg] N NextMsg Spc NextPage U Undelete F Forward
```

Figure 6-6. Pine message index

The main part of the window is a list of the messages in the folder, one message per line. If a line starts with N, like the second message does, it's a new message that hasn't been read before. (The first message has been sitting in the inbox for some time now ...) Next on each line is the *message number*; messages in a folder are numbered 1, 2, and so on. That's followed by the date the message was sent, who sent it, the number of characters in the message (size), and finally the message subject.

At the bottom of the display is Pine's reminder list of commands. When you aren't sure what to do, this is a good place to look. If you don't see what you want here, pressing O (the letter "o"; lowercase is fine) shows you more choices. For more information, ? gives detailed help.

Let's skip this first message and read the next one, number 2. The down-arrow key or the N key moves the highlight bar over that message. As usual, you can get the default action—the one shown in brackets at the bottom of the display (here, [ViewMsg])—by pressing RETURN or > . The message from Jerry will appear.

Just as > took us forward in Pine, the < key generally takes you back to where you came from—in this case, the message index. You can type R to reply to this message, F to forward it (send it on to someone else), D to mark it for deletion, and TAB to go to the next message without deleting this one.

When you mark a message for deletion, it stays in the folder message index, marked with a D at the left side of its line, until you quit Pine. Type Q to quit. First Pine asks if you really want to quit. If you've marked messages for deletion, Pine asks if you want to *expunge* ("really delete") them. Answering Y here actually deletes the message.

There's much more to Pine than we can cover here. For instance, it lets you organize mail in multiple folders, print, pipe (output) messages to Unix programs, search for messages, and more. Recent versions of Pine can access mail folders on other computers using IMAP; this lets you use Pine (and other email programs) on many computers, but keep one main set of mail folders on a central computer.

Sending Email with Pine

If you're sending a quick message from a shell prompt, you may want to use the method shown in the section "Sending Mail from a Shell Prompt" earlier in this chapter. For a more interactive way to send email, try Pine. We'll take a quick tour.

If you've already started Pine, you can compose a message from many of its displays by typing C . (Though, as always, not every Pine command is

available at every display.) You can also start from the main menu. Or, at
a shell prompt, you can go straight into message composition by typing
"**pine** *addr1 addr2*", where each *addr* is an email address like
jerry@oreilly.com. In that case, after you've sent the mail message, Pine
quits and leaves you at another shell prompt.

When you compose a message, Pine puts you in a window called the
composer. (You'll also go into the composer if you use the Reply or Forward commands while you're reading another mail message.) The composer is a lot like the Pico editor, but the first few lines are special
because they're the message *header*—the "To:", "Cc:" (courtesy copy),
"Attchmnt:" (attached file), and "Subject:" lines. Figure 6-7 shows an example, already filled in.

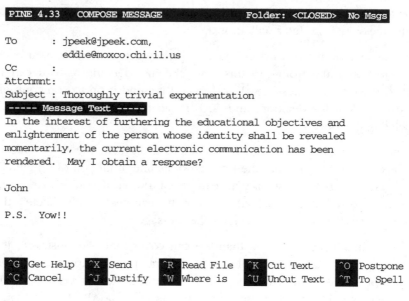

Figure 6-7. Pine composer

As you fill in the header, the composer works differently than when
you're in the message text (body of the message). The list of commands at
the bottom of the window is a bit different in those cases, too. For
instance, while you edit the header, you can attach a file to the end of the
message with the "Attach" command, which is CTRL-J . However, when
you edit the body, you can read a file into the place you're currently editing (as opposed to attaching it) with the CTRL-R "Read File" command.
But the main difference between editing the body and the header is the
way you enter addresses.

If you have more than one address on the same line, separate them with commas (,). Pine will rearrange the addresses so there's just one on each line, as shown in Figure 6-7.

There are several ways to give the composer the addresses where the message should be sent:

- Type the full email address, like *jpeek@jpeek.com.*

- If you're sending email to someone who uses the same computer you do, type their username. Pine will fill in @hostname as soon as you move the cursor to the next line.

- Type a nickname from the address book. (See "the section "Pine address book," later in this chapter.)

Move up and down between the header lines with CTRL-N and CTRL-P , or with the up-arrow and down-arrow keys, just as you would in Pico. When you move into the message body (under the "Message Text" line), type any text you want. Paragraphs are usually separated with single blank lines.

 If you put a file in your home directory named *.signature* (the name starts with a dot, "."), the composer automatically adds its contents to the end of every message you compose. (Some other Unix email programs work the same way.) You can make this file with a text editor like Pico, or from the Pine setup menu (see the section "Configuring Pine," later in this chapter). It's good Internet etiquette to keep this file short—no more than four or five lines, if possible.

You can use familiar Pico commands such as CTRL-J to justify a paragraph and CTRL-T to check your spelling. When you're done, CTRL-X ("exit") leaves the composer, asking first if you want to send the message you just wrote. Or CTRL-C cancels the message, though you'll be asked if you're sure. If you need to quit, but don't want to send or cancel, the CTRL-O command postpones your message; then, the next time you try to start the composer, Pine asks whether you want to continue the postponed composition.

Pine address book

The Pine *address book* can hold peoples' names and addresses, as well as a *nickname* for each person. When you compose a message, enter peoples' nicknames in the message header; Pine replaces that with the full name and address.*

You can enter information by hand from the main menu by choosing [A] ("address book"), then adding new entries and editing old ones. Also, as you read email messages that you've received, the [T] ("take address") command makes new address book entries for that message's addressees.

Figure 6-8 shows the address book entry form. Edit each line as you would in the composer, then use [CTRL-X] to save the entry. The "Fcc" line gives the name of an optional Pine folder; when you send a message to this address book entry, Pine puts a copy in this folder. (If you leave "Fcc" blank, Pine uses the *sent-mail* folder.) All lines except nickname and address are optional.

```
Nickname  : Jerry
Fullname  : Jerry Peek
Fcc       : authors
Comment   : Writes books about Unix and the Internet
Addresses : jpeek@jpeek.com
```

Figure 6-8. Pine address book entry

Once you've saved that address book entry, if you go into the composer and type the nickname *Jerry*, here's the header you get automatically:

```
To       : Jerry Peek <jpeek@jpeek.com>
Cc       :
Fcc      : authors
Attchmnt:
Subject :
```

Configuring Pine

The Pine main menu (shown in Figure 6-5) has a Setup entry for configuring Pine. We assume that your system staff has configured important options, like your printer command, and we look at a few other settings you might want to change.

---

* Recent versions of Pine also let you store your address book on a central server, in order for you to access it, from whatever other computer you're using at the moment, via IMAP.

After you enter $\boxed{\text{S}}$ (the "Setup" command), you can choose what kind of setup you want to do. From the setup screen, you can get to the option configuration area with $\boxed{\text{C}}$ (the "Config" command).

The configuration screen has page after page of options. You can page through them with the space bar (to move forward one page), the $\boxed{-}$ key (back one page), the $\boxed{\text{N}}$ key (to move forward to the next entry), and the $\boxed{\text{P}}$ key (back to the previous entry). If you know the name of an option you want to change, you can search for it with $\boxed{\text{W}}$ (the "Whereis" command).

When you highlight an option, the menu of commands at the bottom of the screen will show you what can do with that particular option. A good choice, while you're exploring, is the $\boxed{?}$ ("Help") command, to find out about the option you've highlighted. There are several kinds of options:

- Options with variable values: names of files, hostnames of computers, and so on. For example, the *personal-name* option sets the name used in the "From:" header field of mail messages you send. The setup entry looks like this:

```
personal-name       = <No Value Set: using "Robert L. Stevenson">
```

  "No Value Set" can mean that Pine is using the default from the system-wide settings, as it is here. If this user wants his email to come from "Bob Stevenson," he could use the $\boxed{\text{C}}$ ("Change Val") command to set that name.

- Options that set preferences for various parts of Pine. For instance, the *enable-sigdashes* option in the "Composer Preferences" section puts two dashes and a space on the line before your default signature. The option line looks like this:

```
[X]  enable-sigdashes
```

  The "X" means that this preference is set, or "on." If you want to turn this option off, use the $\boxed{\text{X}}$ ("Set/Unset") command to toggle the setting.

- For a few options, you can choose one of many possible settings. The option appears as a series of lines. For instance, the first few lincs of the *saved-msg-name-rule* option look like this:

```
saved-msg-name-rule     =
            Set    Rule Values
            ---    ----------------------
            (*)    by-from
            ( )    by-nick-of-from
```

```
( )   by-nick-of-from-then-from
( )   by-fcc-of-from
( )   by-fcc-of-from-then-from
```

The "*" means that the *saved-msg-name-rule* option is currently set to *by-from*. (Messages will be saved to a folder named for the person who sent the message.) If you wanted to choose a different setting— for instance, *by-fcc-of-from*—you'd move the highlight to that line and use the ⟨*⟩ ("Select") command to choose that setting.

These settings are trickier than the others, but the built-in help command ⟨?⟩ explains each choice in detail. Start by highlighting the option name (here, *saved-msg-name-rule*) and reading its help file. Then look through the settings' names, highlight one you might want, and read its help file to see if it's right for you.

When you exit the setup screen with the ⟨E⟩ command, Pine asks you to confirm whether you want to save any option changes you made. Answer ⟨N⟩ if you were just experimenting or aren't sure.

Exercise: sending and reading mail

You can practice sending and reading mail in this exercise:

List logged-in users.	Enter **who**
Choose a user you know, else choose yourself; send a short message to that person using **mail** or your favorite email program.	Enter **mail** *username* or **pine** *username* or . . .
Read the message or messages you got.	Enter **pine** or start your favorite email program; use its "read message" commands.
Reply to one of the messages. (It's okay to reply to a message from yourself.)	Press **R** in **pine** or use your email program's "reply" command. Send the completed reply.
Forward one of the messages. (It's okay to forward a message to yourself.)	Press **F** in **pine** or use your email program's "forward" command. Add a sentence or two of explanation above the forwarded message. Send the completed message.

Usenet News

Usenet, also called "Net News," has thousands of worldwide discussion groups. Each discussion is carried on as a series of messages in its own *newsgroup*. A newsgroup is named for the kind of discussion that happens there. Each message is a lot like an email message. But, instead of being sent to a list of email addresses, a newsgroup message is sent to all the computers that subscribe to that particular newsgroup—and any user with access to that computer can read and reply to the message.

 Because Usenet is a public forum, you'll find a variety of people with a variety of opinions—some impolite, rude, or worse. Although most users are friendly and helpful, a few people seem to cause most of the problems. Until you're accustomed to Usenet, be aware that you may be offended.

To read Usenet groups, you'll need a *newsreader* program, also called a *news client.* Many email programs can read news, too. You can use any newsreader; the principles of all are about the same. Some of the more popular Unix newsreaders are **slrn**, **nn**, and **trn**. We show how to read news with Pine Version 4.33.* If you haven't used Pine before, please read the section "Reading Email with Pine," earlier in this chapter.

If your system's copy of Pine has been set up to read Usenet messages, when you choose the $\boxed{L}$ key ("folder list") from the main menu, you'll get a Collection List screen like Figure 6-9. A *collection* is a group of folders. A collection can be email folders from your local computer, email folders from other computers, or Usenet newsgroup folders. Figure 6-9 shows two collections: *Mail* and *News on news/nntp*. The News collection is selected (highlighted).

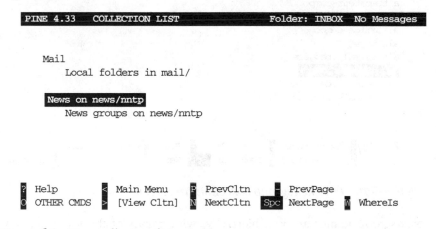

Figure 6-9. Pine collection list screen

---

* Much older versions of Pine can't show newsgroups. Choose another newsreader or upgrade to the newest Pine.

If your copy of Pine is recent enough to read Usenet, but doesn't seem to do it, check the configuration settings, as described in the section "Configuring Pine," earlier in this chapter. The *collectionList* settings can set up a collection of folders for news. You may also need to set the *nntp-server* hostname to the computer which serves news articles; your system staff should be able to tell you the right hostname.

When you press ENTER or > to view that collection, you'll get a list of newsgroup folders that's probably huge. Usenet has something for everyone! The Pine D command will delete a newsgroup from your list; it won't appear anymore unless you use the A command to add it back. (Pine also has some advanced features, like "zooming" to a list of folders that you've defined. See the Pine help system for details.) Figure 6-10 shows a list of some newsgroups.

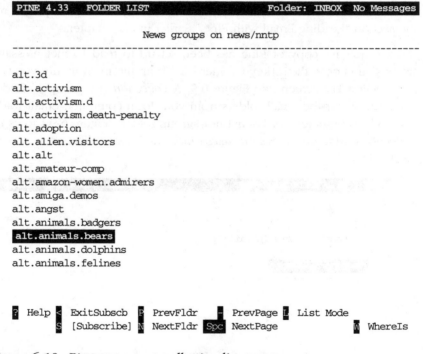

Figure 6-10. Pine newsgroup collection list screen

Newsgroup names are in a hierarchy, with names of the levels separated by dots (.):

•   The main hierarchies include *comp* (for discussions about computers); organization, city, regional and national groups (such as *ne* for New England, *uk* for the United Kingdom, and so on); *misc* ("miscellaneous"); and so on. The *alt* ("alternative") hierarchy is for almost anything that doesn't fit in the others.

- All the top levels have subcategories, or second-level categories. For instance, the *alt* category has subcategories *alt.3d*, *alt.activism*, *alt.adoption*, and so on, as you can see in Figure 6-10.

- A second-level category may have third-level categories. For instance, the category *alt.animals* is divided into *alt.animals.badgers*, *alt.animals.bears*, and so on.

 When you first start to read Usenet, it's a good idea to spend a couple of hours exploring what's available and what you're interested in—and deleting unwanted newsgroups from your list. The time you spend at first will pay you back later, by letting you go straight to the newsgroups in which you're interested.

People all over the world frequent particular newsgroups. Just as mail folders have email messages, newsgroups have *news articles* (individual messages posted by someone). These messages *expire* after a period of time. (That's part of why a lot of newsgroups appear empty.) Let's look into a newsgroup. Go to the newsgroup *news.announce.newusers*; scroll through the folder list by pressing the space bar, or if in a hurry, use the $\boxed{W}$ ("whereis") command and enter the newsgroup name. Once you've selected the name from the collection list, press $\boxed{ENTER}$ or $\boxed{>}$ to view it. You'll see a list of messages in the group, as in Figure 6-11.

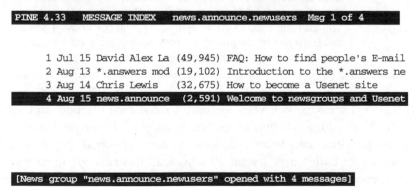

```
PINE 4.33    MESSAGE INDEX    news.announce.newusers   Msg 1 of 4


      1 Jul 15 David Alex La (49,945) FAQ: How to find people's E-mail
      2 Aug 13 *.answers mod (19,102) Introduction to the *.answers ne
      3 Aug 14 Chris Lewis   (32,675) How to become a Usenet site
      4 Aug 15 news.announce (2,591) Welcome to newsgroups and Usenet




[News group "news.announce.newusers" opened with 4 messages]
? Help        < FldrList   P PrevMsg   - PrevPage  D Delete
O OTHER CMDS  > [ViewMsg]   N NextMsg  Spc NextPage U Undelete
```

Figure 6-11. Pine newsgroup message index screen

Read Usenet messages just as you read email messages; for example, select a message from the message index and press ENTER or > to view it. It stays in the index until it's deleted or expires. Deleting messages you've read or don't want to see makes it easier to find new messages that come in later. To keep a message, save a copy to a Pine mail folder with the S ("save") command, email a copy to other users with the F ("forward") command, or save a copy to a file with the E ("export") command.

Remember that people worldwide will see your message and have your email address. If your message is insulting, long and rambling, includes a lot of the original message unnecessarily, or just makes people unhappy, you're likely to get a lot of email about it. Many newsgroups have periodic FAQ ("frequently asked questions") postings that give more information about the group and answer common questions. We suggest that you not post messages to newsgroups until you've read Usenet for a while, have learned what style is acceptable, and have seen enough of the discussion in a particular group to know whether your question or comment has been discussed recently.

Also, remember that spammers (people who send "junk email" with advertising and worse) will be able to see the email address on your Usenet posting. For that reason, many people set a different email address in the "From:" field when posting Usenet messages. If your Internet provider gives you multiple email addresses, you could choose one just for your Usenet postings. (Readers may want to reply to your message by email, though, so consider using an email address that you do read occasionally. You also can include your "real" address in the body of the article, possibly disguised to fool spammers who search Usenet articles for email addresses.)

If there's a message you want to reply to, the Pine R command starts a reply. After asking whether to include a copy of the original message in your reply, Pine asks you: "Follow-up to news group(s), Reply via email to author or Both?" If you want all who read this newsgroup to see your reply, choose F to follow up; your reply, including your name and email address, is posted for everyone to see. If your message is just for the author—for instance, a question or a comment—replying by email with R is the better choice.

You can post a new message to a newsgroup with the [C] ("compose") command. If you're viewing a news folder, Pine asks if you want to compose a message to that newsgroup. (If you answer [N] ("no"), Pine creates a regular email message.)

Here's one more tip: to read expired messages or search through years of archives, web sites like Google Groups (*http://groups.google.com/*) allow this.

Interactive Chat

Need a quick answer from another user without sending an email message and waiting for his reply? Want to have a conversation with your Internet-connected friend in Chile but don't have money for an international phone call? An interactive chat program lets you type text to another user and see her reply moments later. Chatting, or "instant messaging," has become popular recently. Widely known chat programs are available for Unix; as of this writing, those include Jabber and AOL Instant Messenger. Other programs have been available on Unix systems for years. We look at two of these: **talk** and IRC.

talk

The **talk** program is simple to use. Give the username (and, optionally, the hostname) of the person you want to chat with. Then **talk** will try to notify that person as well as show how to use **talk** to complete the connection with you. Both of your terminal windows will be split into two sections, one for the text you type and the other for the text you get from the other person. You can type messages back and forth until one of you uses [CTRL-C] to break the session.

One advantage of **talk** is its simplicity; if each of you has a terminal window open, either of you can run the program at any time; if the other person is logged in, he is notified that you want to chat and told how to complete the connection. If both people want to use **talk** on the same computer—even if one of them is logged in remotely (see the section "Remote Logins," earlier)—it should work well. Unfortunately, there are several **talk** versions that don't work with each other. So, the first time you try to chat with someone on another host, which might have another **talk** version (or other problems), it can take planning. Use an email message or phone call to alert them that you'll try **talk**ing soon, then experiment to be sure that both of you have compatible **talk** systems. After that, you're all set.

Here's the syntax:

> **talk** *username@hostname*

If the other user is logged onto the same computer as you, omit the *@hostname*. After you run that command, your screen clears with a line of dashes across the middle. The top half shows text you type and informational messages about the connection. The bottom half shows what the other user types.

For example, if your username is *juan*, you're logged onto the computer *sandya.unm.edu*, and you want to talk to the user *ana* at the computer *cielo.cl*, you would type "**talk ana@cielo.cl**". If the connection works, your screen clears and you'll see something like Figure 6-12.

```
[No connection yet]
[Waiting for your party to respond]
[Waiting for your party to respond]
[Connection established]
Hi, Ana!  Need any help with your exam?




--------------------------------------------------------------
```

Figure 6-12. A successful talk connection

The message *[Waiting for your party to respond]* means that your **talk** program has found *ana*'s system and is waiting for her to respond. Ana's terminal bell should ring and she should see a message like this in one of her terminal windows:

```
Message from Talk_Daemon@sandya.unm.edu at 18:57 ...
talk: connection requested by juan@sandya.unm.edu.
talk: respond with:  talk juan@sandya.unm.edu
```

If she answers by typing **talk juan@sandya.unm.edu**, the connection should be completed, and her screen should clear and look like Juan's. What she types appears on the top half of her screen and the bottom half of Juan's, and vice versa. It's not always easy to know when the other person has finished typing; one convention is to type *o* (for "over") when you want a response; type *oo* (for "over and out") when you're finished. The conversation goes on until one person types CTRL-C to actually break the connection.

Unfortunately, because there are several versions of **talk**, and because other things can go wrong, you may see other messages from the **talk** program. One common message is *[Checking for invitation on caller's machine]*, which usually means that you won't be able to connect. If this happens, it's possible that one system has other versions of the **talk** program that will work with the particular system you're trying to connect to—try the **ntalk** program, for instance. It might also be easier to use a more flexible chat system, such as IRC.

IRC

IRC (Internet Relay Chat) is a long-established system for chatting with other users worldwide. IRC is fairly complex, with some rules you need to understand before using it. We give a brief introduction here; for more details, see *http://www.irchelp.org*.

Introducing IRC

Unlike the **talk** program, IRC programs let you talk with multiple users on multiple channels. Channels have names, usually starting with "#", such as *#football*. (You might hope that a channel name would tell you what sort of discussions happen there, but you'd often be wrong!) Many channels are shared between multiple servers on an IRC *net*, or network; you connect your IRC program to a nearby server, which spreads your channel to other servers around the net. Some channel names start with "&"; these channels are local to their server, and not shared around the net. Finally, you can meet a user from a channel and have a private conversation, a "DCC chat," that doesn't go through servers.

Each user on a channel has a *nick*, or nickname, which is up to 9 characters long. It's a good idea to choose a unique nick. Even when you do, if someone else with the same nick joins a channel before you do, you must choose another nick.

Two kinds of users are in control of each channel. *Ops*, or channel operators, choose which other users can join a channel (by "banning" some users from joining) and which users have to leave (by "kicking off" those users). If a channel is empty, the first user to join it is automatically the channel op. (As you can imagine, this system means that some ops can be arbitrary or unhelpful. If an op treats you badly, though, you can just go join another of the thousands of IRC channels.) *IRC ops*, on the other hand, are technical people in charge of the servers themselves; they don't get involved with "people issues."

IRC not only lets you chat; it lets you share files with other users. This can be helpful, but it also can be dangerous; see the Warning later in this section.

There are many IRC programs, or "clients," for different operating systems. They all work with each other, though some have more features. The best known Unix program is ircII, which you run by typing **irc**. Another well-liked program, based on ircII, is **bitchx**; get it from *http://www.bitchx.org*. Many programs can be modified by using *scripts* or *bots*; there are thousands of these floating around IRC. But we advise you to use only well-known programs, and to avoid scripts and bots, unless you know that they're safe.

IRC started long before graphical programs were popular. IRC programs use commands that start with a slash (/), such as **/join #football** or **/whois StevieNix**. Some IRC programs have buttons and menus that run commands without typing, but you'll probably find that learning the most common commands is easy—and makes chatting faster, overall, than using a mouse.

IRC can be a wide open security hole if you don't use it carefully. If you type the wrong command or use an insecure program or script, any user can take over your account, delete all of your files, and more. Be careful!

IRC programs can be corrupted; scripts and bots can easily do damage. Even if you think that one is widely known and safe, it can contain a few lines of dangerous "trojan horse" code added by an unscrupulous user. Also, never type a command that another IRC user suggests unless you're sure you know what it does; **/load** and **/dcc get** can be especially dangerous.

Finally, you should know that IRC users can get information about you with the **/whois** *nick* command, where *nick* is your current nick. They'll see your real name unless you set the IRCNAME environment variable to another name (and log into your system again to make the change take effect). This is explained in the section "Customizing Your Account," in Chapter 3. (By the way, use **/whois** with your nick to find out what other people can see about you.)

A sample IRC session

When you type **irc**, your terminal screen splits into two parts. The top part shows what's happening on the server and the channel; the bottom part (a single line) is where you type commands and text. In between the two parts is a status line with the time of day, your nick, and other information. Some terminals can't do what **irc** wants them to; if you get an error message about this, try the command **irc –d** to use "dumb mode" instead.

A good ircII command to start with is **/help**, which provides a list of other commands. The commands **/help intro** and **/help newuser** give introductions. For help with a particular command, give its name—such as **/help server** for help with the **/server** command. When you're done with help, you'll get a "Help?" prompt; you can type another help topic name, or simply press RETURN to leave the help system. Another common command is **/motd**, the "message of the day," which often explains the server's policies.

You can type your nick on the **irc** command line. Your IRC program should have a default server. You can change servers with the **/server** command; you'd do this if your server is full (you get the message "connection timed out," "connection refused," etc.). If your default IRC server is down or busy, you can also give a server hostname on the **irc** command line, after your nick.

In the following examples, we show the text you type (from the bottom line of the screen) in **boldface**, followed by the responses you might see (from the top of the screen) in unbolded text.

```
$ irc sstjohn us.undernet.org
*** Connecting to port 6667 of server us.undernet.org
    ...
*** Closing Link: sstjohn by austin.tx.us.undernet.org (Sorry, your
+connection class is full - try again later or try another server)
*** Connecting to port 6667 of server us.undernet.org
    ...
*** Welcome to the Internet Relay Network sstjohn (from
+Arlington.VA.US.Undernet.Org)
    ...
*** on 1 ca 1(4) ft 10(10)

/motd
*** The message of the day was last changed: 27/7/2001
*** on 1 ca 1(4) ft 10(10)
*** - Arlington.VA.US.Undernet.Org Message of the Day -
*** - 27/7/2001 20:39
    ...
*** -               SERVER POLICIES:
```

```
    ...

/help newuser
*** Help on newuser
    ...
*** Hit any key for more, 'q' to quit ***
    ...
Help? RETURN

/whois sstjohn
*** sstjohn is ~jpeek@kumquat.jpeek.com (Steve St. John)
*** on irc via server *.undernet.org (The Undernet Underworld)
*** sstjohn has been idle 1 minutes
```

Messages from the server start with ***. Long lines are broken and continue on following lines that start with +. After connecting to the server, I
used **/whois** with my nick to find what information other users could see
about me. The Undernet servers have thousands of channels open, so I
started by searching for channels with "help" in their names; you can use
wildcards, such as **help**, to do this:

```
/list *help*
*** Channel    Users  Topic
*** #helpmania 2      A yellow light, an open door, hello neighbor,
+there's room for more. English
*** #underneth 14     -= UndernetHelp =- Ask your color free questions
+& wait for it to be answered. (undernethelp@fivemile.org)
*** #mIRCHelp  14     Welcome to Undernet's mIRC Help Channel! Beginners
+welcome :-)
*** #irc_help  48     Welcome to #irc_help. We do not assist in
+questions/channels regarding warez, mp3, porn, fserve, etc.
    ...list goes on and on...

/list *mp3*
    ...list of groups discussing/sharing MP3 files...
```

I want to see what's happening, so I join the biggest help channel:
#irc_help, which has 48 users now:

```
/join #irc_help
*** sstjohn (jpeek@kumquat.jpeek.com) has joined channel #irc_help
*** Topic for #irc_help: Welcome to #irc_help. We do not assist in
+questions/channels regarding warez, mp3, porn, fserve, etc.
*** Users on #irc_help: sstjohn ChuckieCheese Dodgerl GooberZ
+Kinger MotorMouth @theDRJoker MrBean SweetPea LavaBoy GrandapaJoe
    ...
```

Some names in the list of users, like *@Darkmind*, start with @; these users
are ops. Let's watch some more of the action. After a couple of users leave

the channel, a new user *MsTiger* joins and asks for help. Each time a user types a line of text that isn't a command, it's sent to everyone else on the channel, preceded by that user's nick, like *<MsTiger>*:

```
*** ChuckieCheese has left channel #irc_help
*** GooberZ has left channel #irc_help
*** HelloWorld (~hw@foo.edu) has joined channel #irc_help
*** MsTiger (~tiger@zz.ro) has joined channel #irc_help
<MsTiger> help me
<MsTiger> please
<Kinger> MsTiger what can we help you with ?
<MsTiger> my channel is not op
<Kinger> LavaBoy tell MsTiger about no opers
<LavaBoy> MsTiger, *shrug*
<GrandapaJoe> MsTiger Sorry, but there are currently NO IRC Operators
+available to help you with your channels. Please be patient and wait
+for an Operator to join.
*** MsTiger has left channel #irc_help
```

The channel has gotten quiet, so I jump in with a question:

```
Hello all. When I joined, I had a problem
    ...
Any suggestions??
*** Thor (dfdddd@194.999.231.00) has joined channel #irc_help
<[Wizard]> Can you help me plz
<LavaBoy> Try typing !help in the channel, [MORTAL].
/leave
*** sstjohn has left channel #irc_help
/quit
$
```

No one had an answer, so I left the channel after a few minutes of waiting. Other channels might be a lot livelier, and might have had someone willing to chat about my question, but I left the irc program by typing /quit. Then I got another shell prompt.

7

In this chapter:
* *Running a Command in the Background*
* *Checking on a Process*
* *Cancelling a Process*

Multitasking

Unix can do many jobs at once, dividing the processor's time between the tasks so quickly that it looks as if everything is running at the same time. This is called *multitasking*.

With a window system, you can have many applications running at the same time, with many windows open. But most Unix systems also let you run more than one program inside the *same terminal*. This is called *job control*. It gives some of the benefits of window systems to users who don't have windows. But, even if you're using a window system, you may want to use job control to do several things inside the same terminal window. For instance, you may prefer to do most of your work from one terminal window, instead of covering your desktop with multiple windows.

Why else would you want job control? Suppose you're running a program that will take a long time to process. On a single-task operating system such as MS-DOS, you would enter the command and wait for the system prompt to return, telling you that you could enter a new command. In Unix, however, you can enter new commands in the "foreground" while one or more programs are still running in the "background."

When you enter a command as a background process, the shell prompt reappears immediately so that you can enter a new command. The original program will still run in the background, but you can use the system to do other things during that time. Depending on your system and your shell, you may even be able to log off and let the background process run to completion.

Running a Command in the Background

Running a program as a background process is most often done to free a terminal when you know the program will take a long time to run. It's used whenever you want to launch a new window program from an existing terminal window—so that you can keep working in the existing terminal, as well as in the new window.

To run a program in the background, add the "&" character at the end of the command line before you press the RETURN key. The shell then assigns and displays a process ID number for the program:

```
$ sort bigfile > bigfile.sort &
[1] 29890
$
```

(Sorting is a good example because it can take a while to sort huge files, so users often do it in the background.)

The process ID (PID) for this program is 29890. The PID is useful when you want to check the status of a background process, or if you need to, cancel it. You don't need to remember the PID, because there are Unix commands (explained in later sections of this chapter) to check on the processes you have running. Some shells write a status line to your screen when the background process finishes.

Here's another example. If you're using a terminal window, and you'd like to open another terminal window, you can probably click a button or choose a menu item to do that. But, if you occasionally want to specify command-line options for that new window, it's much easier to type the options on a command line in an existing window. (Most menus and buttons don't give you the flexibility to choose options each time you open a new window.) For instance, by default, an **xterm** window saves 64 lines of your previous work in its "scrollback buffer." If you'll be doing a lot of work that you'll want to review with the scrollbar, you might want to open a new window with a 2000-line scrollback buffer. You could enter the following command in an existing **xterm** window:

```
$ xterm -sl 2000 &
[1] 19283
```

A new **xterm** window should pop open—where you'll be able to scroll almost forever.

In the C shell, you can put an entire sequence of commands separated by semicolons (;) into the background by putting an ampersand at the end of the entire command line. In other shells, enclose the command sequence in parentheses before adding the ampersand. For instance, you might want to sort a file, then print it after **sort** finishes. The syntax that works on all shells is:

> (*command1; command2*) &

The examples above work on all shells. On many systems, the shells have the feature we mentioned earlier called *job control.* You can use the *suspend character* (usually CTRL-Z) to suspend a program running in the foreground. The program pauses and you get a new shell prompt. You can then do anything else you like, including putting the suspended program into the background using the **bg** command. The **fg** command brings a suspended or background process to the foreground.

For example, you might start **sort** running on a big file, and, after a minute, want to send email. Stop **sort**, then put it in the background. The shell prints a message, then another shell prompt. Send mail while **sort** runs.

```
$ sort hugefile1 hugefile2 > sorted
        ...time goes by...
CTRL-Z  Stopped
$ bg
[1]     sort hugefile1 hugefile2 > sorted &
$ mail eduardo@nacional.cl
        ...
```

Checking on a Process

If a background process takes too long, or you change your mind and want to stop a process, you can check the status of the process and even cancel it.

ps

When you enter the command **ps**, you can see how long a process has been running, the process ID of the background process and the terminal from which it was run. The **tty** program shows the name of the terminal where it's running; this is especially helpful when you're using a window system or you're logged into multiple terminals. Example 7-1 shows this in more detail.

Example 7-1. Output of ps and tty programs

```
$ ps
   PID TTY       TIME CMD
 27285 pts/3    0:01 csh
 27285 pts/3    0:01 ps
 29771 pts/2    0:00 csh
 29792 pts/2    0:54 sort
$ tty
/dev/pts/3
```

In its basic form, **ps** lists the following:

Process ID (PID)
> A unique number assigned by Unix to the process.

Terminal name (TTY)
> The Unix name for the terminal from which the process was started.

Run time (TIME)
> The amount of computer time (in minutes and seconds) that the process has used.

Command (CMD)
> The name of the process.

In a window system, each terminal window has its own terminal name. Example 7-1 shows processes running on two terminals: *pts/3* and *pts/2*. Some versions of **ps** list only the processes on the same terminal where you run **ps**; other versions list processes on all terminals where you're logged in. If you have more than one terminal window open, but all the entries in the TTY column show the same terminal name, try typing either "**ps x**" or "**ps -u** *username*", where *username* is your username. If you need to find out the name of a particular terminal, run the **tty** program from a shell prompt in that window, as shown in Example 7-1.

While using a window system, you may see quite a few processes you don't recognize; they're probably helping the window manager do its job. You may also see the names of any other programs running in the background and the name of your shell's process (**sh**, **csh**, and so on)—although different versions of **ps** may show fewer processes by default. **ps** may or may not list its own process.

You should be aware that there are two types of programs on Unix systems: directly executable programs and interpreted programs. Directly executable programs are written in a programming language such as C or Pascal and stored in a file that the system can read directly. Interpreted programs, such as shell scripts and Perl scripts, are sequences of commands that are read by an interpreter program. If you execute an interpreted program, you will see an additional command (such as **perl**, **sh**, or **csh**) in the **ps** listing, as well as any Unix commands that the interpreter is executing now.

Shells with job control have a command called **jobs** which lists background processes started from that shell. As mentioned earlier, there are commands to change the foreground/background status of jobs. There are other job control commands as well. See the references in the section "Documentation" in Chapter 8.

Cancelling a Process

You may decide that you shouldn't have put a process in the background. Or you decide that the process is taking too long to execute. You can cancel a background process if you know its process ID.

kill

The **kill** command aborts a process. The command's format is:

> kill *PID(s)*

kill terminates the designated process IDs (shown under the PID heading in the **ps** listing). If you do not know the process ID, do a **ps** first to display the status of your processes.

In the following example, the "**sleep** *n*" command simply causes a process to "go to sleep" for *n* number of seconds. We enter two commands, **sleep** and **who**, on the same line, as a background process.

```
$ (sleep 60; who)&
[1] 21087
$ ps
 PID    TTY   TIME  COMMAND
20055    4    0:10  sh
21087    4    0:01  sh
21088    4    0:00  sleep
21089    4    0:02  ps
$ kill 21088
[1]+  Terminated              sleep 60
$ tom     tty2   Aug 30  11:27
grace    tty4   Aug 30  12:24
tim      tty5   Aug 30  07:52
dale     tty7   Aug 30  14:34
```

We decided that 60 seconds was too long to wait for the output of **who**. The **ps** listing showed that **sleep** had the process ID number 21088, so we used this PID to kill the **sleep** process. You should see a message like "terminated" or "killed"; if you don't, use another **ps** command to be sure the process has been killed.

The **who** program is executed immediately, since it is no longer waiting on **sleep**; it lists the users logged into the system.

Problem checklist

The process didn't die when I told it to.

> Some processes can be hard to kill. If a normal kill of these processes is not working, enter "**kill -9** *PID*". This is a sure kill and can destroy almost anything, including the shell that is interpreting it.

> In addition, if you've run an interpreted program (such as a shell script), you may not be able to kill all dependent processes by killing the interpreter process that got it all started; you may need to kill them individually. However, killing a process that is feeding data into a pipe generally kills any processes receiving that data.

8

Where to Go from Here

Now that you're almost to the end of this guide, let's look at some ways to continue learning about Unix. Documentation is an obvious choice, but it isn't always in obvious places. You can save time by taking advantage of other shell features—aliases, functions, and scripts—that let you shorten a repetitive job and "let the computer do the dirty work."

We'll close by seeing how you can use Unix commands on non-Unix systems.

Documentation

You might want to know the options to the programs we've introduced—and get more information about them and the many other Unix programs. You're now ready to consult your system's documentation and other resources.

The man Command

Different versions of Unix have adapted Unix documentation in different ways. Almost all Unix systems have documentation derived from a manual originally called the *Unix Programmer's Manual*. The manual has numbered sections; each section is a collection of manual pages, often called "manpages"; each program has its own manpage. Section 1 has manpages for general Unix programs such as **who** and **ls**.

Many Unix installations have individual manual pages stored on the computer; users can read them online. If your system has online manpages, and you want to know the correct syntax for entering a command or the

410.634 UNIX Lab 3

410.634 Johns Hopkins University

Name: _____

UNIX Lab 3 and *vi* text editor

Drills:

1. Do the exercises on p. 96 …and then try these:

ps -ef | grep "yourname"
compress users
zcat users.Z
uncompress users.Z

2. Copy the following 5 files from ~jgreene/vilearn-1.0 (**/users/spon/asptg/0/.jgreene/vilearn-1.0**) to your home directory:

1basics , 2moving, 3cutpaste, 4inserting, and 5tricks

Use **vi** on each file to do the tutorial on files 1, 2, 3, and 4 - go as far as you can in one hour's time. If you don't finish, do it from home/work.

Exercises - turn in at beginning of next week's class.

1. Put the output from the **date** command into a file **now.txt**. What command did you use?

date > now.txt

2. Append the output from **who** to the **now.txt** file. What command did you use?

who >> now.txt

3. Connect the **who** and **sort** commands with a pipe (you may also need to use **more**). Who is the first user on the list?

4. **cd ~jgreene/bin** and use grep to find which files were last modified in September.

5. Type **ps**. What commands are you running?

6. What is the output from **uname -a** ? What UNIX version are we using?

7. Use the **man** command to look up the **wc** command. What does this command tell you, in order?

8. Use **vi** to edit **~jgreene/WC1953.txt** file (copy it to your home directory first; one paragraph - don't panic! You can view the text of this article at http://biocrs.biomed.brown.edu/Books/Chapters/Ch%208/DH-Paper.html).

particular features of a program, enter the command **man** and the name of the command. The syntax is:

man *command*

For example, if you want to find information about the program **mail**, which allows you to send messages to other users, enter:

```
$ man mail
       .
       .
$
```

The output of **man** may be filtered through a pager like **less** automatically. If it isn't, just pipe the output of **man** to **less** (or **more** or **pg**).

After you enter the command, the screen fills with text. Press SPACE or RETURN to read more, and q to quit.

Some systems also have a command called **apropos** or **man -k** to help you locate a command if you have an idea of what it does but are not sure of its correct name. Enter **apropos** followed by a descriptive word; you'll get a list of commands that might help.

Problem checklist

man *says there is no manual entry for the command.*
> Some commands—**cd** and **jobs**, for example—aren't separate Unix programs; they're part of the shell. On some Unix systems, you'll find documentation for those commands in the manual page for the shell. (To find the shell's name, see the section "The Unix Shell" in Chapter 1.)

> If the program isn't a standard part of your Unix system—that is, your system staff added the program to your system—there may not be a manual page, or you may have to configure the **man** program to find the local manpage files.

The info Command

Linux systems, as well as some others, have a program called **info**. It serves the same purpose as **man**: to document system programs. The **info** output is in a different format, though. The syntax to start **info** is:

info *command*

For example, if you want to find information about the program **find**, which searches for files, enter **info find**. After you enter the command, press SPACE to read more or "q" to quit.

Documentation via the Internet

The Internet changes so quickly that any list of online Unix documentation we'd give you would soon be out of date. Still, the Internet is a great place to find out about Unix systems. Remember that there are many different versions of Unix—so some documentation you find may not be completely right for you. Also, some information you'll find may be far too technical for your needs (many computer professionals use and discuss Unix). But don't be discouraged! Once you've found a site with the general kind of information you need, you can probably come back later for more.

Many Unix command names are plain English words, which can make searching hard. If you're looking for collections of Unix information, try searching for the Unix program named **grep**. As this book went to press, one especially Unix-friendly search engine was Google, at *http://www.google.com*.

Here are some other places to try:

- **Magazines**, both in print and online-only, have Unix tutorials and links to more information. Many are written for beginners.

- **Publishers**, like O'Reilly & Associates, Inc. (*http://www.oreilly.com*), have areas of their websites that feature Unix and have articles written by their books' authors. They may also have books online (such as the O'Reilly Safari service) available for a small monthly fee—which is a good way to learn a lot quickly without needing to buy a paper copy of a huge book, most of which you may not need.

- **Vendors' sites** like Red Hat (*http://www.redhat.com*), and Unix-related organizations like the Free Software Foundation (*http://www.fsf.org*), usually have documentation and support files online, where you can search for what you need.

- **Universities** often use Unix-like systems and will have online documentation. You'll probably have better luck at the Computer Services division (which services the whole campus) than at the Computer Science department (which may be more technical).

Books

Bookstores, both traditional and online, are full of computer books. The books are written for a wide variety of needs and backgrounds. Unfortunately, many books are rushed to press, written by authors with minimal Unix experience, full of errors. Before you buy a book, read through parts of it. Does the style (brief or lots of detail, chatty and friendly or organized as a reference) fit your needs? Search the Internet for reviews; online bookstores may have readers' comments on file.

Shell Aliases and Functions

If you type command names that are hard for you to remember, or command lines that seem too long, you'll want to learn about *shell aliases* and *shell functions*. These shell features let you abbreviate commands, command lines, and long series of commands. In most cases, you can replace them with a single word or a word and a few arguments. For example, one of the long pipelines the section "Pipes and Filters" (Chapter 5) could be replaced by an alias or function named (for instance) "aug." When you type **aug** at a shell prompt, the shell would list files modified in August, sorted by size.

Making an alias or function is almost as simple as typing in the command line or lines that you want to run. References in the section "Documentation," earlier in this chapter, have more information. Shell aliases and functions are actually a simple case of shell programming.

Programming

We mention earlier that the shell is the system's command interpreter. It reads each command line you enter at your terminal and performs the operation that you call for. Your shell is chosen when your account is set up.

The shell is just an ordinary program that can be called by a Unix command. However, it contains some features (such as variables, control structures, and so on) that make it similar to a programming language. You can save a series of shell commands in a file, called a *shell script*, to accomplish specialized functions.

Programming the shell should be attempted only when you are reasonably confident of your ability to use Unix commands. Unix is quite a powerful tool and its capabilities become more apparent when you try your hand at shell programming.

Take time to learn the basics. Then, when you're faced with a new task, take time to browse through references to find programs or options that will help you get the job done more easily. Once you've done that, learn how to build shell scripts so that you never have to type a complicated command sequence more than once.

You might also want to learn Perl. Like the shell, Perl interprets script files full of commands. But Perl has a steeper learning curve than the shell. Also, since you've already learned a fair amount about the shell and Unix commands by reading this book, you're almost ready to start writing shell scripts now; on the other hand, Perl will take longer to learn. But if you have sophisticated needs, learning Perl is another way to use even more of the power of your Unix system.

Using Unix on Non-Unix Systems

Once you get comfortable working quickly at the Unix command line, you may miss that power and flexibility when you use another system like Microsoft Windows. You can get programs—both commercial and freely available—that let you use a Unix-like shell prompt and Unix utilities (**grep**, **sort**, and so on) from within other operating systems. You'll also find that an increasing number of systems are built on top of the stable Unix or a Unix-like operating system. Two of the latest examples are Mac OS X on the Macintosh and a variety of machines with Linux embedded inside.

 Unix, Microsoft Windows, and the Macintosh all use different conventions for the way that they mark the end of a line of text. If you transfer text files between these systems, you'll probably need to convert them. (The command-line FTP client does this automatically if you set its ascii transfer mode.) And if you have an executable program file that runs on one system, it won't run on the others—unless it's written in Java or it's a *script* program from a language such as the shell or Perl.

Under Microsoft Windows

Cygwin, from *http://www.cygwin.com*, is a package of Unix-like software development utilities that runs under Microsoft Windows NT, 98, and 95 (and probably others, as Microsoft Windows evolves). Although it's aimed at software developers, it also has a lot of the standard Unix utilities. You can use Cygwin from its **bash** shell (a Unix-like shell) or from the standard Windows command shell.

The *MKS Toolkit*, from *http://www.mks.com*, is a commercial package of Unix-like utilities that runs under Microsoft Windows. MKS Toolkit has been on the market, and been updated constantly, since the time of MS-DOS in the 1980s.

With a little hunting, you'll find versions of other Unix programs for Windows systems. Three of these are the Pine email program, the Lynx browser, and **vim**, a version of the **vi** text editor.

Mac OS X

The latest version of the Macintosh operating system (as of this writing) is Mac OS X, a Unix-based system. The OS X window system, Aqua, interacts with the operating system much as the X Window System you've seen in this book. (In fact, you now can use X on the Mac!)

If you want to use a Unix-like terminal under OS X, you can open Terminal. It's a regular double-clickable application found in */Applications/Utilities*. Navigate to it using the Finder, launch it, and you'll get a terminal window like the ones shown in this book.

Once you open Terminal, you can use standard Unix utilities on your Mac files, on files you create with those utilities, or on files you transfer over a network. File pathnames are separated by slashes (/), just as on Unix, but be sure to put quotes around Mac filenames that don't follow our file naming rules (see the section "File and Directory Names" in Chapter 4). Unlike Unix and Windows, some Macintosh files have two *forks*: the resource and data forks. If you copy a Mac file, watch out—the **cp** utility won't copy both forks! Instead, you'll need to install and run **CpMac** (from the Developer Tools CD that comes with OS X; then you can simply run **/Developer/Tools/CpMac**).

Glossary

alphanumeric
> Characters: letters (*alpha*) and numbers (*numeric*), including punctuation characters (such as _ and ?).

click
> Depress and quickly release a mouse button; double- and triple-click imply depressing and releasing a mouse button two or three times, respectively, within a short period. You'll usually click with the first mouse button (which is the left mouse button for righthanded users—or the opposite if your mouse has been configured for a lefthanded user). See also *point.*

clipboard
> A temporary storage area for X Window System programs, used for transferring text ("copying" and "pasting" text) between programs.

command
> A command is an instruction that you can give to a program running on the Unix system. For instance, you can type a program's name and arguments on a command line, at a shell prompt; this command asks the shell to run that program. (The shell is a program itself; see *shell.*) Once a program starts running, it may accept commands of its own. For example, a text editor has commands for deleting and adding text to the file it's editing.

> The terms *command* and *program* are used almost interchangeably, probably because the program name is typed first on a command line (at a shell prompt). Shells have some *built-in* commands that don't start a separate program running; one of these is **cd**, which changes the shell's working directory.

cracker
> A malicious person who tries to break into computer systems (usually via a network), disrupt computers and networks, steal secrets (like passwords and credit card numbers), and other antisocial behavior.

Popular media often call these people *hackers*. But, to most computer programmers, a hacker is someone who enjoys computing and programming, and may be an expert at some area of it. (For instance, a *Perl hacker* is someone who's good at programming in the Perl language.)

desktop
> The part of a display that's "behind" (not enclosed within) the windows, icons, and other items on the display. Also called the *root window*.

directory
> A list of files and/or other directories. A directory is actually a special kind of file that has names and locations of other files and directories. See also *working directory*.

display
> One meaning of *display* is to make something visible, as in "the command displays its result." In the X Window System, a *display* is the viewable area output by the X *display server*. Usually this is a single terminal screen, but X can be configured to use multiple screens as part of the same display.
>
> Multiscreen X displays aren't common, though, and sentences like "the result is displayed on the display" are clumsy. To avoid confusion, we use the term *screen* for the visual output of your computer—whether it's an alphanumeric terminal or a graphical workstation. See also *screen*.

drag
> As in *drag an object*, i.e., a window or an icon, means to point to the object and then depress and hold down (usually) the first mouse button while moving the pointer to a new location, where the mouse button is released.
>
> Some Unix desktop environments support "drag and drop," which means dragging one object and dropping it over another object. For example, to print a file, you could drag the file's icon and drop it onto a printer icon.

Free Software Foundation (FSF)
> An organization formed in 1985 that works for the right of computer users to study, copy, modify, and redistribute computer programs. The FSF also distributes free software. See *http://www.fsf.org/*; see also *GNU*.

GNOME
> A project to develop a free desktop environment (a window system and more) for free operating systems. See *http://www.gnome.org/*; see also *KDE*.

GNU
> A project, started in 1984, to develop a completely free Unix-like operating system: the GNU system. GNU stands for "GNU's Not Unix"; it is pronounced "guh-NEW." See also *Free Software Foundation*.

KDE
  A desktop environment (a window system and more), as well as a family of
  application programs, for Unix-like workstations. See *http://www.kde.org/*; see
  also *GNOME.*

mouse pointer
  The graphic symbol that appears on the output display and moves under the
  control of the mouse, trackball, or keyboard input to the window system.

  In the X Window System, the pointer is actually called a *cursor.* But we use
  the term "pointer" in this book to distinguish the cursor under control of the
  mouse from other cursors that you'll sometimes see (such as the "I-beam" cursor in an **xterm** window).

multitasking
  An operating system that can run more than one program at a time is said to
  be a *multitasking OS.* The programs don't actually all run simultaneously: the
  OS can divide the computer's time between the different programs, very
  rapidly, so that they all *appear* to run at the same time. The system can still
  be overloaded, and run slowly, if too many programs are trying to run at
  once.

  Unix has always been multitasking. MS-DOS (an early Microsoft OS) was not.

pathname
  The location of a file or directory in a Unix filesystem: a series of names separated by slash (/) characters. Pathnames can be *absolute* (starting with a slash
  character, which means they begin at the filesystem's root directory) or *relative* (not starting with a slash, which means the pathname starts from the current working directory). See also the section "The Unix Filesystem" in Chapter
  3.

point
  As in "point a mouse," means to position the mouse pointer at a specified
  place or location within a window or other part of a window system display.
  See also *click, drag.*

program
  A set of instructions to the computer, written by a programmer, and stored in
  a file. The program is executed when you type its name as the first word on a
  command line, at a shell prompt—or when you choose the program from a
  menu or icon in a window system. Unix runs a program as a *process*, which
  you can suspend or terminate using job control, an interrupt key, or the **kill**
  command.

root (user and directory)
  Unix systems have an account named *root*, also called the "superuser," that
  has no protections or restrictions. System administrators and staff use this
  account to make changes to the system's configuration and operation.

A Unix filesystem is like an upside-down tree with a branching structure of directories inside directories. The first directory, where the filesystem starts, is called the *root directory*. Figure 3-1 is a filesystem diagram showing the root directory and a small part of a filesystem.

screen

The area of a terminal (usually glass or plastic) that shows computer output. See also *display* and *terminal.*

session

When two programs, or two users running programs, communicate across a network, they typically start the communication by doing a certain thing—for instance, by logging in. The communication continues until it's completed (or, possibly, aborted before it completes)—for instance, by logging out. The entire process, from start to completion, is called a *session.*

shell

A program that runs other programs. There are several different kinds of shells, each with its own command-line syntax; some of the most common are **bash**, **tcsh** and **ksh**. All shells do the same basic job: reading commands that you type interactively at a shell prompt, or reading commands noninteractively from a program file called a *shell script.*

When you start using a terminal (by logging in) or a terminal window (by starting a program such as **xterm**), a shell program begins to run and prints a shell prompt. When you terminate that shell (by typing **exit** or $\boxed{\text{CTRL-D}}$ at a prompt), you're logged out from that terminal; a terminal window will close.

syntax

The rules for, or the format of, the characters you use to make a command or other computer input. For example, the syntax of a Unix command line is explained in the section "Syntax of Unix Command Lines" of Chapter 1.

terminal

Computer hardware that provides a way to input data to, and display output from, an operating system and programs running under it. Usually the input hardware is a keyboard and the output is a glass or plastic screen. For the purposes of this book, there are two types of screens or terminals, *alphanumeric* and *graphical.*

An alphanumeric terminal can only display text, can't run a window system, and usually doesn't have a mouse or other pointing device.* An alphanumeric terminal displays alphanumeric characters—and possibly simple graphics (lines, boxes and maybe a few special symbols). An alphanumeric terminal can't handle a window system and typically doesn't have a mouse or other pointing device; if the cursor can be moved around the screen, it's probably done with arrows or other keys on the keyboard. See also *alphanumeric.*

---

* Before the widespread use of glass terminals (when data transmission rates were slow) it was common to use a teletype as both the input and output hardware. This is why Unix terminals are often called *ttys*.

A graphical terminal can usually run a window system—with arbitrary-sized windows, images (photographs and other graphics), sound, etc. Graphical terminals are typically *bitmapped*, which means that each *pixel* (dot of color) can be individually controlled by the computer—as opposed to an alphanumeric terminal, where the terminal itself chooses which dots to turn on and off to make letters, numbers, and other characters that the computer has told it to create.

terminal window

A window, on a window system, made by a terminal emulation program such as **xterm**, GNOME Terminal, or **konsole**. It's an interface like an alphanumeric terminal—with a shell prompt where you can type command lines from your keyboard and can see any text that those programs output. In most cases, a mouse or other pointing device is useless inside a terminal window—though it works at the borders of the window (to minimize the window, move it, etc.) just as on other windows.

titlebar

The part of the window border above a window. It shows the window's title. It also has buttons and/or menus that control characteristics of the window, such as minimizing the window or lowering the window to the bottom of a window stack. Figure 2-4 shows a titlebar.

virtual consoles

Virtual consoles, available on Linux and other PC operating systems, let you access several different fullscreen login sessions on the same screen, independent of any window system. Just after a reboot, if you get a "login:" prompt (as in Example 1-1), you'll be using the first virtual console. To use other virtual consoles, hold down the ⌷CTRL⌷ key and the left ⌷ALT⌷ key, then press one of the function keys ⌷F1⌷ (for the first console) through ⌷F6⌷ (for the sixth). Each of those function keys will bring up a separate login session. (Once you've started the X Window System, ⌷CTRL⌷-⌷ALT⌷-⌷F7⌷ may take you to the X display.) Use each virtual console for whatever you want—just remember to log out of each when you're done!

window

An area of an output display often smaller in size than the maximum size of the display screen.

If a window manager program is running, a window usually will have a well-defined border, a title, and other characteristics. The window manager lets you move and resize a window as well.

working directory

When you give Unix a *relative* pathname to a file or subdirectory, the working directory is the starting point—the directory where that relative pathname starts. Here are two examples:

If your working directory is */home/joe/food* and you type the command **less recipes/fish**, Unix opens the file */home/joe/food/recipes/fish*. (Your working directory is still */home/joe/food*.)

If you type the command "**ls ..**" from any working directory, you get a listing
of the files in your parent directory. That command uses the relative pathname to the parent directory (..). So if your working directory is */home/joe/
food*, that command would list the parent directory */home/joe*. Or, if your
working directory is */home/joe*, that same command would list the parent
directory */home*.

Each process running on a Unix system has its own working directory, which
the program can change at any time. For instance, you can give the shell the
command **cd** to change its working directory.

x86 processor
Since the 1980s, the Intel Corporation has been building a family (series) of
microprocessors (which are used in computer *CPUs*, Central Processing Units)
whose model numbers end in the number 86. The first was the 8086; then
came the 80286 (the 80186 wasn't as widely used); next was the very popular
80386; and so on. Many operating systems run only on a certain family of
microprocessors. Microsoft Windows, for instance, is primarily designed for
the x86 family; recent versions won't work on a processor earlier than the
80586. Unix-like operating systems run on many different microprocessor fam-
ilies, but the x86 is one of the most popular—especially for Linux, which
works well with an 80386.

xterm program
A program that runs under the X Window System. It makes a terminal window (called an xterm window) in which a Unix login session runs.

Index

Symbols

& (ampersand)
  background processes and, 131
  IRC, using, 125
  starting the window manager
    and, 21
< (input redirection operator), 87
> and >> (output redirection
    operator), 88-91
* (asterisk)
  executable files and, 53
  wildcards, 58, 67, 79
| (pipe) for I/O redirection, 88
[] (bracket), as wildcards, 68
^ (caret), cutting or copying text in
    pico, 72
: (colon) as a less prompt, 55
- (hyphen) for command options, 11
$ (dollar sign), as shell prompt, 4, 6,
    21
. (dot)
  directory shortcuts, 46, 50, 76
  in filenames, 66
= (equal sign) operator, 58
(hash mark)
  using IRC, 125
  as shell prompt, 6

% (percent sign), as shell prompt, 21
; (semicolon)
  background commands,
    running, 132
  command lines and, 12
/ (slash)
  IRC, using, 126
  ls command and, 53
  pathnames and, 45-47
  root directories and, 43, 46
? (question mark), as a wildcard, 67
?word command (less), 55

A

-a (all) option, (ls), 50
absolute pathnames, 45, 46
access modes (permissions), 51, 57
accounts (Unix), 1-11, 42-65
  customizing, 63-65
address book (Pine), 116
aliases (shell), 139
alphanumeric terminals, 17
ampersand (&)
  background processes and, 131
  IRC, using, 125

We'd like to hear your suggestions for improving our indexes. Send email to
index@oreilly.com.

About the Author

Jerry Peek has used Unix since the early 1980s. He has consulted on Unix and VMS, developed and taught Unix courses, been a staff writer for O'Reilly & Associates, Inc., and worked as a programmer and system administrator.

Grace Todino (Gonguet) is now a "professional expatriate," having lived in Oman, Gabon, and Holland for the last 10 years. She currently resides in Sarawak (Malaysia) with her geophysicist husband, Christophe, and their children, Gabriel, Raphael, and Lucie. Grace was one of the original authors of the Nutshell Handbooks *Managing UUCP and Usenet* and *Using UUCP and Usenet*. She now writes and edits travel articles for local publications.

John Strang is an Assistant Professor of Diagnostic Radiology at the University of Rochester, Rochester, NY. His research interests are in CAT scan and MRI of the body, as well as in computerization of radiologic images. He received his education at MIT (BS and MS), Northwestern Medical School (MD), and UCLA and Stanford (post-graduate medical training).

Colophon

Our look is the result of reader comments, our own experimentation, and feedback from distribution channels. Distinctive covers complement our distinctive approach to technical topics, breathing personality and life into potentially dry subjects.

The animal on the cover of *Learning the Unix Operating System* is a horned owl. The horned owl is the most powerful of North American owls, measuring from 18 to 25 inches long. This nocturnal bird of prey feeds exclusively on animals—primarily rabbits, rodents, and birds, including other owls. It locates these animals by sound rather than sight, since its night vision is little better than ours. To aid its hunting, an owl has very soft feathers that muffle the sound of its motion, making it virtually silent in flight. A tree-dwelling bird, it generally chooses to inhabit the old nests of other large birds such as hawks and crows, rather than build its own nest.

Mary Brady was the production editor and copyeditor for *Learning the Unix Operating System*. Linley Dolby and Claire Cloutier provided quality control. Joe Wizda wrote the index.

Edie Freedman designed the cover of this book, based on her own series design.The cover image is a 19th-century engraving from the Dover Pictorial Archive. Emma Colby produced the cover layout with QuarkXPress 4.1, using Adobe's ITC Garamond font.

David Futato designed the interior layout based on a series design by Nancy Priest. The print version of this book was created by translating the DocBook XML markup of its source files into a set of gtroff macros using a filter developed at O'Reilly & Associates by Norman Walsh. Steve Talbott designed and wrote the underlying macro set on the basis of the GNU *troff*–*gs* macros; Lenny Muellner adapted them to XML and implemented the book design. The GNU groff text formatter Version 1.11.1 was used to generate PostScript output. The text and heading fonts are ITC

Garamond Light and Garamond Book. The illustrations that appear in the book were produced by Robert Romano and Jessamyn Read using Macromedia FreeHand 9 and Adobe Photoshop 6.

Whenever possible, our books use a durable and flexible lay-flat binding.

Other Titles Available from O'Reilly

Unix Basics

Learning the Korn Shell, 2nd Edition

By Bill Rosenblatt, Arnold Robbins
2nd Edition April 2002
432 pages, ISBN 0-596-00195-9

Learning the Korn Shell is the key to gaining control of the Korn shell and becoming adept at using it as an interactive command and scripting language. Readers will learn how to write many applications more easily and quickly than with other high-level languages. A solid offering for many years, this newly revised title inherits a long tradition of trust among computer professionals who want to learn or refine an essential skill.

UNIX in a Nutshell: System V Edition, 3rd Edition

By Arnold Robbins
3rd Edition September 1999
616 pages, ISBN 1-56592-427-4

The bestselling, most informative Unix reference book is now more complete and up-to-date. Not a scaled-down quick reference of common commands, UNIX in a Nutshell is a complete reference containing all commands and options, with descriptions and examples that put the commands in context. For all but the thorniest Unix problems, this one reference should be all you need. Covers System V Release 4 and Solaris 7.

Learning the bash Shell, 2nd Edition

By Cameron Newham &
Bill Rosenblatt
2nd Edition January 1998
336 pages, ISBN 1-56592-347-2

This second edition covers all of the features of bash Version 2.0, while still applying to bash Version 1.x. It includes one-dimensional arrays, parameter expansion, more pattern-matching operations, new commands, security improvements, additions to ReadLine, improved configuration and installation, and an additional programming aid, the bash shell debugger.

Using csh and tcsh

By Paul DuBois
1st Edition August 1995
242 pages, ISBN 1-56592-132-1

Using csh and tcsh describes from the beginning how to use these shells interactively to get your work done faster with less typing. You'll learn how to make your prompt tell you where you are (no more pwd); use what you've typed before (history); type long command lines with few keystrokes (command and filename completion); remind yourself of filenames when in the middle of typing a command; and edit a botched command without retyping it.

Learning GNU Emacs, 2nd Edition

By Debra Cameron, Bill Rosenblatt & Eric Raymond
2nd Edition September 1996
560 pages, ISBN 1-56592-152-6

Learning GNU Emacs is an introduction to Version 19.30 of the GNU Emacs editor, one of the most widely used and powerful editors available under Unix. It provides a solid introduction to basic editing, a look at several important "editing modes" (special Emacs features for editing specific types of documents, including email, Usenet News, and the World Wide Web), and a brief introduction to customization and Emacs LISP programming. The book is aimed at new Emacs users, whether or not they are programmers. Includes quick-reference card.

Learning the vi Editor, 6th Edition

By Linda Lamb & Arnold Robbins
6th Edition October 1998
348 pages, ISBN 1-56592-426-6

This completely updated guide to editing with vi, the editor available on nearly every Unix system, now covers four popular vi clones and includes command summaries for easy reference. It starts with the basics, followed by more advanced editing tools, such as ex commands, global search and replacement, and a new feature, multi-screen editing.

How to stay in touch with O'Reilly

1. Visit our award-winning web site

http://www.oreilly.com/

★ "Top 100 Sites on the Web"—PC Magazine
★ CIO Magazine's Web Business 50 Awards

Our web site contains a library of comprehensive product information (including book excerpts and tables of contents), downloadable software, background articles, interviews with technology leaders, links to relevant sites, book cover art, and more. File us in your bookmarks or favorites!

2. Join our email mailing lists

Sign up to get email announcements of new books and conferences, special offers, and O'Reilly Network technology newsletters at:

http://www.elists.oreilly.com

It's easy to customize your free elists subscription so you'll get exactly the O'Reilly news you want.

3. Get examples from our books

To find example files for a book, go to:

http://www.oreilly.com/catalog

select the book, and follow the "Examples" link.

4. Work with us

Check out our web site for current employment opportunites:

http://jobs.oreilly.com/

5. Register your book

Register your book at:
http://register.oreilly.com

6. Contact us

O'Reilly & Associates, Inc.
1005 Gravenstein Hwy North
Sebastopol, CA 95472 USA
TEL: 707-827-7000 or 800-998-9938
      (6am to 5pm PST)
FAX: 707-829-0104

order@oreilly.com
For answers to problems regarding your order or our products. To place a book order online visit:

http://www.oreilly.com/order_new/

catalog@oreilly.com
To request a copy of our latest catalog.

booktech@oreilly.com
For book content technical questions or corrections.

corporate@oreilly.com
For educational, library, and corporate sales.

proposals@oreilly.com
To submit new book proposals to our editors and product managers.

international@oreilly.com
For information about our international distributors or translation queries. For a list of our distributors outside of North America check out:

http://international.oreilly.com/distributors.html

O'REILLY®